Wings Like Eagles

David Marfleet is a remarkable pilot.

At 20, the youngest helicopter pilot in the newly formed Army Air Corps, he learned operational flying the hard way—with the parachute Regiment in Northern Ireland, overseas in the desert and later with the SAS.

Soldier first and pilot second, he flew with a machine-gun under his seat, aware that death could face him at any moment. The shocking loss of a comrade affected him deeply.

Still more testing was flying the high mountain valleys of remote Irian Jaya, where David's calling led him next.

The climax of his unique career came when called on to rescue hundreds of villagers from the jaws of an earthquake, a highly dangerous mission which prompted his special flying award.

Clive Langmead is a writer, producer and broadcaster. Born in Nairobi, Kenya, he has spent much of his life travelling. After an early career sailing the world as a ship's navigating officer, his more recent work has been for the BBC in Europe, Africa and the United States, first as a journalist, then as a presenter for Radio 4 and producer for BBC Television. Now independent, he runs his own production and training company, *Langmedia*, with his wife Elizabeth. They have three sons and live an unquiet life in the Malvern Hills.

Wings Like Eagles

Clive Langmead

A LION BOOK

Copyright © 1991 Clive Langmead

Published by
Lion Publishing plc
Sandy Lane West, Oxford, England
www.lion-publishing.co.uk
ISBN 0 7459 2119 1

First edition 1991
10 9 8 7 6 5 4

A catalogue record for this book is available
from the British Library

Printed and bound in Great Britain
by Cox & Wyman Ltd, Reading

Contents

Foreword

I first met David Marfleet across a BBC microphone. I was recording a series of interviews for Radio 4, and from the moment we first shook hands he struck me as a remarkable personality, and likely to be a very relaxed interviewee with something to say. He was also plainly a man who had really lived through all that he talked about. Not just, in the broadcasters' jargon, 'a good talker', but 'a good doer' as well.

David's wide smile and irrepressible good humour (even in studio) hid some very sober and solid facts. He had once been a dedicated paratrooper and army helicopter pilot, blooded in the front line of the bitter battlefield of Northern Ireland, and had served later with the SAS anti-terrorist squad. Leaving the army, he had chosen to continue flying helicopters in one of the most professionally challenging and remote regions of the world—the primary jungles, mountains and rivers that make up Irian Jaya, in South-east Asia.

What he was doing there made up the substance of a fascinating radio interview, and is now the basis for this book, the fruit of a hope sparked off by that first meeting in 1985. Five years later, he left Irian Jaya with his family to return to Britain. This, his story, is the result of many interviews over the last few months.

But Moondi, whom you will also encounter in these pages, I have never met. Nor has anyone, for he doesn't exist. I wrote his character into the story as a way of showing something of the impact aircraft had, and continue to have, on the many complex stone-age cultures of South-east Asia. He does not exist but he is, nevertheless, wholly authentic, as are his family. And his Hupla people do very much exist; they have been through precisely all that this story reveals. Here I must thank local language expert and translator John Wilson for his help and detailed advice.

In fact Moondi is not quite fictional: his is an amalgam of several real characters, and to fully authenticate this, my concluding chapter is taken directly from a letter written to David Marfleet from a former colleague, Sue Trenier, a nurse in the Desa Valley, the home of the Hupla.

The other liberty I have taken, in trying to relate not only the facts but the spirit of David's energetic life, is with military radio procedure. Radio conversations are part of flying, and military aircraft in particular are controlled and directed from the ground a great deal. But these transmissions are, of necessity, curt, cryptic and concise. A message such as 'Alpha Two One Charlie, this is Three Niner, commence serial Zero Zero Seven. Out.' could mean anything from an order secretly dispatching SAS paratroops on a raid, to announcing the end of a map-reading exercise. I decided therefore that some of the radio work needed 'unpacking' when it came to writing. To an outsider the bare military communication conveys nothing (as is intended), but to the recipient it is full of meaning. I have tried to record the sense of this, as much as the words used.

As David would say, in his forthright manner: 'If you want a story full of numbers then go out and read a phone book!' But now please let me introduce to you one of the most remarkable pilots I have been privileged to interview, on the air or in it: David Marfleet.

Clive Langmead, Malvern

1
The Jump

For the first time in my life I was scared. Scared absolutely rigid. Waves of fear broke over me as I stood waiting.

The RAF flight sergeant had seen it all before. He smiled cheerfully. 'We *are* going to be ready to jump now, aren't we, sir?'

I nodded, glassy-eyed.

'Not too much of an ordeal now, sir. We've done it once before. Only eight hundred feet and you're there. No problem, sir.'

I nodded again. His patronizing approach galled me. Army officers are not patronized by anyone. Let alone RAF flight sergeants.

He looked at the other three in the balloon basket, swaying gently on its winch cable over No. 1 Parachute Training School, RAF Abingdon. They could be divided into two groups. Fearless, confident, steel-eyed paratroopers-to-be. And me—Lieutenant Marfleet, Army Air Corps.

The irony was that I had probably had more time in the air than all of them put together. A fully trained combat helicopter pilot and infantry officer, blooded under fire in Northern Ireland. But the plain truth was, I was terrified of heights.

I thought back to my 'P Company' Parachute Regiment basic selection course. This inclined towards the masochistic to say the least. Much of the time was spent struggling over cold and rain-swept Welsh hilltops. That was bad enough, but what had really fazed me was the paratroop assault course in Farnborough. Leaping from muddied plank to muddied plank suspended at tree-top height. Eighty feet up. I tried not to look down. Paratroops must spend a lot of their time up in trees, I had concluded. Nevertheless I had got through. But I just had that feeling that worse was to follow. I was right. 'P Company' was tough, but I hadn't feared it. I was never afraid. Yet now I was absolutely petrified.

'P Company' was to see if you could hack it as a soldier. But then you had to get your parachute wings. Teaching this business was the province of the RAF. And they knew their business. For two weeks we had rolled and tumbled in parachute harness from various wooden frames set on the walls of hangars. We learned how to jump out of—or, as they put it, 'make an exit' from—a mock-up fuselage. We learned how to land. We learned how to fall over. We learned how to get up again. We learned how to control a 'canopy' or 'PX military parachute'. In fact, we learned all the essentials of leaving a perfectly serviceable aircraft, in no danger or trouble, relying for support solely on an overgrown silk handkerchief. And hoping to hit the ground as soon as possible so as to be ready to be shot at from all sides by the enemy. What a way to go to war.

But right now the practice was over. The first jump was also over. For me, it had been something of a philosophical exercise. I had ignored everything except the immediate commands of the instructor. Ignored the balloon, ignored the height, just jumped. The sense of plummeting helpless through the air was wholly unnerving, and none of the training had, nor could have, prepared me for it. My exit had been lousy, and the landing horrible. But first jumps are always like that, so they say.

With the second jump you know what you are in for. My eyes had been opened, and I was terrified. Nothing in

10

'P Company' had prepared me for it. All my training, all my soldiering. It really wasn't important. Nothing was. Only getting out of that balloon alive.

In the mountains of Irian Jaya, it was the hour of first light. The stone-age tribesman squatted ruminatively at the entrance to his wood-and-thatch hut. The dwellings of his people, the Hupla, were set in a series of small groups on the sloping flanks of a deep long valley. Soba. Home to the Hupla people.

Each hut was placed a short distance from a neat, stone-walled garden, where the family cultivated its staple diet of sweet potatoes. Now, outside each home, waiting, squatted the head of the house. Waiting for the sun.

A hazy blue light suffused the valley, smoky from the cooking fires of yesterday, now rekindled for early morning. Mist swirled and rippled up the valley sides, caressing the trees. A cock crowed. Domestic pigs grunted. The tribesman kept his peace. Moondi Jala's eye followed the reaching, fingering lines of mist eastwards to the lightening horizon and a distant range of mountains. The edge of the world. At least, so he had thought as a boy. Now he knew this was not so. There were other peoples out there. Beyond the valleys were many tribes: Dani, Yali, Kimyal, Mek ... so many that most likely no man could ever number them. He had even heard there was a land out there of no valleys at all, where huts could be built on level ground. It was not a pleasing prospect. To be without a valley was unthinkable.

He shivered. Not from the cold. Cold was not within a Hupla's experience. One of the Noble Tribes of the High Valleys, the Hupla liberally applied the recovered fat from that oldest friend of man—the household pig—rubbing it thickly into naked flesh to keep warm in the cold of night and the chill of the morning. There was an uneasy feeling in the air. A sense of something about to happen.

11

Moondi scratched restlessly at his only article of clothing. An enormous, sprouting, dried gourd, which rose up vertically from his loins, placed neatly over and accentuating strikingly his own masculinity. The hollow penis gourd was two feet long, and ended at his breast-bone. Decorated with a feather plume at the top, it was secured by a woven chest strap. It irritated and itched where the cloth band held the rough natural ornament across his chest. But it was a good feeling. It was a manly itch. Gourds came in many subtle sizes and styles—each saying both something about the wearer and the particular work he was about. This morning on rising he had solemnly put aside his short everyday gourd for this present magnificent plume. It was his pride and the pride of his family, worn only on the most important of occasions, when the real work of men was to be done. Today for the first time he wore it for war.

2
War Footing

'All set, sir?' Flight Sergeant Casey held me firmly by the back of my pack. The basket, or possibly me, swayed horrendously. Casey ignored it.

'You're going to need to push me,' I murmured.

'Just remember to look up and smile, sir.' He paused. 'Green on, and GO, sir!'

'Oh, Jesus,' I replied. His firm hand and my collapsing legs got me over the edge. As instructed I looked up to check my canopy was opening, pulled out by the static line attached to the basket. It was. On the first jump I had been transfixed by the ground rushing up to meet me and forgotten. The chute ripped out, Casey's farewell smile receded behind a cloud of white silk, and I pulled into as good a landing position as I could manage in the remaining seconds.

Once down I had no time to rest and recover. Another helpful flight sergeant was hounding me purposefully as I sprawled, a quivering jelly, on the grass.

'Come on, sir! First actions, first actions ... remember! Collapse the canopy. Bundle up, bundle up. Evenly, sir, evenly ... it isn't washing. Now move, sir, MOVE! We don't want boots in our skull, do we, sir?'

No more did we. I skittered sideways with the remains of my chute as another helpless enthusiast plummeted to earth beside me. I gritted my chattering teeth. Two down. Eight to go. Those parachute wings *were* going to be mine.

One day, soon.

If you think Jesus' name came a little readily to my lips you should know two things. First: up there I was *really* scared; and second, that I generally spend quite a bit of time talking to him one way and another. Not that I put his name about lightly. No, but as a Christian, direct dealings with him are something of a routine business. And especially when I'm scared.

In fact, it would be fair to say that I joined up because of Jesus. I always felt, even as a small boy, that I was going to end up a flying Christian missionary. Now, you could say it was my parents' influence, or my natural adventurous spirit that made me want to be a missionary. But I was also convinced my missionary work was likely to involve flying. Yes, well, perhaps that *was* a bit strange. I know a lot of little boys dream of flying, and quite a lot of them are Christians, but there aren't that many who feel that one day they are going to end up flying around for Jesus! Still, there it is. That's how I felt.

More concretely, I had come across an organization formed to develop missionary aviation. It had grown up after—and in a sense out of—the Second World War. A fellowship of trained wartime pilots, who had seen first-hand how aircraft had transformed the face of conflict, could see the possibilities for peace time too. Aircraft could carry personnel safely at speed over rough, hostile and often entirely impassable terrain. It was just what they had been doing for the last five years. It could be a way of supplying isolated out-stations, hospitals, schools and clinics regularly by air. It made sense. They set out to show it could be done.

By the late sixties, an established and effective aerial operation was up and running. To me, young as I was then, this sounded like something worthwhile. So as I came of age I decided I would get trained to fly. First I approached the navy. They liked the cut of my jib, and gave me a flying 'scholarship'. This meant about 35 hours in a Cessna 150, ending with a Private Pilot's Licence. Well, I was on the way. But, when I thought about it, I realized that missionary aviation, certainly then, was mostly about light, single-engine monoplanes flying over jungle or desert. The navy flew mostly heavy, high-speed jets from carriers over the sea. I discarded ideas of a blue suit, and took a look at khaki.

The army Royal Corps of Transport seemed just the thing. They flew the Beaver—a single-engine, high-wing reconnaissance monoplane. These planes, from what I could gather, continually roamed around places like Malaya, Aden, Cyprus and so on. Perfect training for me. Unfortunately the army thought otherwise. Whatever the navy could see in me the army couldn't. As far as they were concerned, I had absolutely no officer potential whatsoever.

So, just to show them, I joined up as a private. And, to cheer up my rather disappointed ('Why-don't-you-go-and-get-a-real-career?') father I joined his old wartime corps: the Royal Engineers. One year of boot-cleaning and bridge-building later, I was an officer candidate for the Royal Corps of Transport. There was just one problem: the Corps had given up Beavers! So I did an about turn, and became one of the first, and youngest, direct-entry officer into the brand new Army Air Corps.

It was more than six months before I even smelt an aircraft. The first thing I was told about being an army pilot was that flying was seen as almost incidental. I was to be a soldier first and a pilot second. My good engineering background with the Sappers was summarily dismissed, and I was sent away to learn how to be a 'real' soldier, an infantry officer with the Royal Hampshires.

It was a high-speed experience. At nineteen I was commanding thirty-two infantrymen, and very soon I learned they would be going into battle—for real.

It was summer leave, and I was the lone orderly officer in the barracks. The phone rang in the Mess.

'Orderly officer.'

'Good. Colonel Hansard here. Operations, UK Land Forces.'

'Sir!'

'Bit of a problem in Ireland blowing up, Lieutenant. Need to recall the battalion. Get on to it, will you?'

'Sir!' The phone clicked. Somewhat stunned, I called the guardroom.

'Corporal Willis? Orderly Office at the double!' As the soldier complied I turned to the classified wall-safe, and withdrew a bulky red sealed package marked 'Live Operational Orders'. I split the seals, and searched for the call-out list.

'Ah, Corporal Willis . . .' I noted excitedly as he puffed through the door. 'Hope you've brought your telephone manner with you. We've got some calling to do. As of now, the battalion's on a war footing—for Northern Ireland!'

He shrugged. 'Nearer the missus than Malaya, sir,' was all he said. And *I* was to lead *him* into battle? I passed the list across. We picked up the phones, and started dialling.

We were dictating urgent telegrams long into the small hours. The battalion straggled back from leave and, shortly after, left for the troubled Province. But I was not included. The Army Air Corps decided that, for me, Northern Ireland could wait. It had a prior commitment—to teach me to fly. Which it did: on a helicopter.

I couldn't believe it. All my time and trouble to get just the sort of flying I wanted—on Beavers—and then this. Helicopters! But the army put its boot down. Airborne forces, we were told, were the troops of the future. Modern soldiers no more expected to walk into battle than Napoleon's cavalry. Indeed, the last war had proved it. In a few short years, every soldier would be air-mobile. In the UK, of course, the RAF had the responsibility of actual transportation but we, the Army Air Corps, were the soldiers' spearhead.

Reconnaissance, observation, command and control,

sighting for the guns, and much, much more. And in this scheme of things, the operational flexibility of the modern helicopter against that of light fixed-wing aircraft had been noted and confirmed. I prayed and I petitioned. But in the end I learnt to fly helicopters. I had done what I reasonably could. I accepted it. I figured if Jesus were organizing, then he probably knew best. So it was to prove. But a lot, lot later.

3
Irian

The mist began to rise steadily through the bluish grey of the valley's dawn. Shredded ribbons of cloud clung to the very tops of the rain forest until the emerging equatorial sun had gained enough strength to burn them away. It was the hour of thought and consideration. The Silence before the activities of the day. It was the time when those who had a mind to could sometimes see ahead, before the pace of events clouded the important issues. A time when sobriety might lead to wisdom and decision for the success of the tribe. Moondi concerned himself with such things, for he was a new warrior, now destined as his father before him to become a tribal High Elder and leader of his people.

Moondi, as were all the men of the High Valleys, was bred for war. It was their honour and their right. The men were the tribe. The womenfolk cooked and sowed and reaped and carried and built and bore children and spun and plaited. But the men's work was war. Glorious were the tales Moondi had been told as a boy. His father and grandfather, his uncles and cousins by the several wives of his father, his more distant tribal relatives, all had told tales of battles of revenge and retribution. Raids and counter-raids.

There were two types of fighting, he knew. Raids were bitter personal disputes when a small group from one tribe set out to capture or kill those of another to settle a difference. Close, bloody, desperate encounters, these happened in jungle and undergrowth near, or inside, another's territory. Moondi had been out on one raid. He had been in the rear, because of his youth. He had heard a lot and seen nothing. The raid had been compromised, and they had had to retreat in a hurry leaving one warrior dead, victim of a clever ambush.

But a raid was not battle. Battle was different. Battle was decisive. Battle was an open, formal affair with strict rules and forms. Battle took place on the open fighting grounds which had been chosen and laid out by their fathers and forefathers before them. It was the manly way to settle differences by bow and spear. Today was a day for battle. And today he knew he would be in the warrior line for the first time. His father had chosen him for the field today. It had been his honoured position to do so. Indeed his father had chosen this battle.

For two seasons a mysterious and deadly sickness had slain many children in the tribe. Moondi himself had lost a younger brother and second cousin. So a Spirit Feast had been called, and the Spirit Talkers of the valley had met and communed together. Then they had presented his father, the High Elder, with the conclusions of their divination and research.

It was apparent that the Hupla from a nearby valley had 'sung a spell' on them. They had taken offence because of a sweet potato blight which had affected them for many months. The cause of this was a disturbed ancestor, whom they had attempted to propitiate by sending one of his great-grandchildren to be with him, by ritual sacrifice. This had failed, so they had re-directed their ancestor's anger on to the Hupla of Moondi's tribe with a Spirit Song.

This had not affected their sweet potatoes much, but the children of Moondi's tribe had begun to suffer. Anybody could see, maintained the Spirit Talkers, that this angry ancestor from another tribe simply wanted more children to be with him. So he was taking them. The sickness could only be halted, they concluded, by calling a formal battle and shedding blood. At worst, this would alert the enemy to their responsibilities, and force them to placate their ancestor properly with some of their own offspring. At best, the shedding of blood might just deal with the problem there and then. It was their ancestor, after all.

It was a complex business which Moondi knew, as his father's son, he would one day have to master. But the conclusion had been straightforward enough, and so messengers had been dispatched to arrange a formal confrontation. His father had chosen the fighting field for the day carefully, once again in consultation with the Spirit Talkers.

There were several regular battle sites spaced out along the line of the valley. These sites were agreed, and had been used for generations between tribes. Each had its advantages and disadvantages. Spiritual, tactical, historical. In choosing the field, his father had recalled who had fought there before, and why; who had been favoured on the day and who defeated; what their ancestral and spiritual status had been at the time; and their entitlement to support from spirit forces. And so on. In the end, his father had chosen (as Moondi knew he would) the location so loved by his grandfather before he died, high up across the valley. Although tactically this would put the tribe at a disadvantage, fighting upwards from the lower slopes, Moondi's father was a pragmatist. Whatever the Spirit Talkers said with all their chants and bones and portents, he knew his own father wouldn't let him down. For Grandfather, hidden up there above it all, would look down and be pleased, and reward them with a kill.

So the challenge messages had gone out, and the warriors had been identified. Not every warrior from each tribe would fight. Only a selected group, loosely backed up by a reserve in case things got desperate. But no tribe would expect to press an advantage. It was against the rules. Sufficient flowing blood would be enough to indicate a clear victory.

Moondi remembered warmly his father's proud smile as he had touched his arm at the War Feast, indicating that this time he was to be one of the chosen. He recalled the kick of his own pulse as he quickly lifted his spear to signify acceptance. It was a moment to savour. For ever. Accepting the responsibility of blood, father to son.

When the sun had risen to the crook of the valley it would be time to go. Moondi shivered again. He could not stop it. He was conscious of a deep conflict within himself. He was looking forward to the battle. He was not afraid of it. His heart was steady. And yet he felt no lightness of spirit. He would, if he could, kill one of the enemy. But the prospect, for some reason, held no allure for him. His soul was in confusion, and he grasped at the short stabbing spear resting by him on the ground.

The stabbing spear was an elegant, rigid, sharpened stick marked with feathers and rings which proclaimed, as did his gourd, his rank and status. It was meant for use in battle but in the formalized battles of the valleys rarely came to use. Most wounding and killing was done by the flights of arrows which sped from front line to front line, raining down upon completely naked and unshielded bodies. At close quarters the long thin throwing spears would be launched. Both, if sighted early by an alert warrior, could be dodged and avoided. Only if vengeance were the driving force would a warrior employ his stabbing spear for a quick hasty thrust to the chest or stomach of an enemy warrior unlucky enough to be disabled away from the effective protection of his comrades. It was always a fatal blow, but often cost a wounding for the assailant who, owing the nature of the encounter, would be likely to be dangerously advanced from his own front line of warriors. Formal battles did not result in many deaths. But those that did were either lingering and dreadful, or quick and bloody.

By now Moondi's aunt had emerged from the hut, and was scratching around in the walled garden. He knew that the sweet potatoes she needed for the men's breakfast were already harvested, cut and prepared. What she really wanted was to see and feel the mood of the dawn silence. See the still, smoking huts each with a fighting man squatting at the entrance. Each calling up their ancestors with the rising sun to encourage them, and steeling themselves for the fray. It heartened her to see it.

Seeing her, Moondi wished it had been his beloved wife, the first wife of his youth, who had just emerged into the garden and not his aunt. He loved his wife. Her grace and beauty. He did not know what love was, but he had heard that very occasionally a special bond developed between men and some of their wives. It was neither expected, nor frequent. But it did happen, and it had happened to him.

His thoughts flew back again to the War Feast. He had loved her especially that night. He remembered watching her through the flickering flames of the fire, as he gorged himself on baked, fatty pork wrapped in banana leaves. He, lolling on the ground, exhausted from dancing. The drums beating heavily, and the women performing a dance in honour of the warriors. She had glanced at him often during it. She was proud to be his wife. He thought she was beautiful. For she was showing she was not afraid.

The night had ended with the Spirit Ceremony, and the wives of the chosen warriors had been lead in turn to the Table of Hands. There, swiftly and skilfully, the Spirit Talkers, assisted by their acolyte tribesmen, had severed a finger from each hand of each girl. He had seen Lanya's body jerk violently at each amputation. Then she had been led away, her mutilated hands bound in banana leaves and ashes from the Cleansing Fire.

He had lain with her that night as the tribal rules

prescribed, and his spirit ancestors demanded, but she had soon fallen into a fever. And her hands would not heal. She was now, six days later, no better. In fact, she was much worse. Vengefully, he ground the butt of his spear into the ground, causing his aunt to look up suddenly.

'Go!' he barked, breaking the silence of the dawn. She rolled her eyes, and scuttled back fearfully into the hut. Moondi was not a man to contradict. His wife's voice, fevered and distant, emerged.

'Moondi. Oh, my warrior, help me!'

Immediately, in one graceful movement, he rose, turned and entered the hut. Tenderly he put his hand on her chest, and called silently on the spirits of his tribe, on the name of his illustrious grandfather, counting up before them, a tally of earnestness, the fingers of his female relatives which had been offered up. He willed her well, shaking with the tension of it, the sweat standing out on his forehead as he forced his wife's spirit up out of her belly whence he knew it had sunk, up into her chest, and over her heart.

If he could move it by his will, by his appeal, then he knew she would recover. He loved her greatly, and could not bear to lose her. As she moaned and tossed, his features grew grim. Now in his heart he knew that his battle would be for her. The touch of his tense and trembling body cheered her, and she reached out her swollen disfigured hands as he bent over her.

'Moondi. Save me!' she repeated.

He knew also that day he would have to kill. He turned and left the hut, squatting down once more at his station by the door.

4

Warriors

'This,' said Instructor Sergeant Farmer, 'is the Bell 47 G4a.' His West Country accent rolled out reassuringly over the group of assembled flying students on the grass dispersal in front of No. 3 Hangar at the Army Air Corps Centre, Middle Wallop, in the Wiltshire countryside on the edge of Salisbury Plain. Army country. Everything was olive green. Everything which moved saluted. Squads of soldiers doubled back and forth. People In Charge stood efficiently with clipboards. And the very air was alive with beating blades and droning engines.

'It is an *American* aircraft,' he continued lightly. 'That is why it looks like a windmill pump which has blown over on the open prairie. I expect that is where Mr Bell got the idea from. On some occasions we wish he hadn't. But by and large, it's OK. The British Army uses it as a basic rotary-wing trainer. Should you by accident learn to fly it, the Army will then let you loose on the Bell 47 G3b Military Variant, also known as the Sioux, which, as you can see there looks like a slightly larger windmill pump...'

Sergeant Farmer was waxing expansive on the subject he knew best. Helicopters were his life, and he had every intention of making them ours. If we failed the course it would not be for his want of trying. We nodded enthusiastically. We were all for wind-pumps, just so long as they flew.

The Sioux and its younger sister the G-4 are probably best known as the machines which the US Army used to evacuate field casualties to the MASH operating theatres in the Korean war. I also remember one appeared regularly on television in a children's adventure series called *Whirlybirds*.

To my eye, the obvious feature was not so much the open tail-rotor spar, which did look rather like the derrick of a wind-pump, but the enormous plexiglass bubble which surrounded the cockpit. It resembled a massive monocular dragonfly on skis. Everything about it was open and exposed: engine, fuel tanks, control runs. An elementary flying machine. So elementary in fact that one of the pre-flight checks was to tap the exposed tail-rotor drive shaft with a coin—to see if it had rusted!

It flew with the aid of a chunky six-cylinder piston engine and a massive two-bladed rotor which was weighted at each end. The rotor carried so much momentum that if you switched off the engine you could still perform a quick hop off the ground with the residual power left in the spinning blades! And I've chopped the odd sapling down with it before now, as well, landing too close to the brush. Nothing worth mentioning in the log-book of course. The army called it the Sioux. We called it the Clockwork Mouse. The way it was built, it looked as if you should put a big winding key in the side to get it started. I soon got to know every click and bump of that machine. Sergeant Farmer saw to that.

Success in helicopter flying is a matter of co-ordination. But it isn't the smooth, comfortable co-ordination you find with a fixed-wing aircraft. It is a matter of wild desperate manoeuvres in a bucking, kicking, living, vibrating bedstead of a machine. There are three main controls. One looks like an over-large brake lever in a car, moves up and down, and effectively controls the power. This is known as the 'collective'. Nothing to do with Soviet agriculture, it collectively adjusts the angle of the rotor blades to the airflow, giving overall lift. On the Bell you had to feed in power by twisting a throttle on the end of the lever to rev the engine, and pulling up it, to increase pitch, at the same time.

Then there is the 'cyclic' or control stick which sits between your legs rather like the joystick in an aeroplane. This controls direction and balance by adjusting the pitch of the blades in a sequential manner. You spend a lot of time stirring that one like a pudding at the start. Well, most of the time, actually.

Finally there are the rudder pedals which decide which way you want the machine to point. They adjust the thrust of the compensating tail rotor. Without it the main rotor would spin one way, and the body of the helicopter the other, which is bad for morale. Over all, it's good policy to point the way you are going, but in a helicopter that isn't mandatory. Which is just another thing to worry about.

The most difficult thing to learn is to stay put, flying nowhere. Hovering. We spent hour after hour wrestling with the controls until we had mastered it. The instructor would sit beside me, and 'release' one set of controls to me at a time. First the collective. I would keep on pulling it up and down, trying to stay just three feet from the ground. Then he would give me the cyclic while he watched the height, and I tried to stay over the small square painted in the grass that was my hover pad, sliding back and forth, stirring away like it was three weeks to Christmas. Then he'd let me have the rudder pedals, and we would spin around like a weathercock in a gale as I tried to boot the machine straight. It took a lot of practice. But I got there in the end.

As I got more proficient, though, Sergeant Farmer developed an annoying habit. Engine-off landings. Half-way through an exercise he would close the throttle without warning, and let me land. A helicopter doesn't crash if the engine stops, but some skill is needed to convert whatever height there is into power as the blades windmill around in auto-rotation. This sort of skill is mandatory to pilots of single-engine helicopters, especially ones that are liable to be shot at. So he was just making sure I kept up the payments on my life assurance. At nineteen I didn't see it that way. I was just irritated. So I paid him back. One day while he was landing, I cut the power on him. Woomph! We slammed into the ground in a barely creditable arrival—right outside the colonel's office.

As the dust settled I noticed a missile heading my way: the C.O. I was about to receive the rocket of all rockets. I draw a veil over the explosion. No, Sergeant Farmer was not amused. The colonel was not amused. No one was amused. By close of play, not even me. I learned later that as far as the colonel was concerned, it was the end of my career there and then. But Sergeant Farmer, having cooled off, had pleaded my case, saying I was an immature adolescent who had received a thorough-going broadside, and that it wouldn't happen again. I have a lot to thank him for. I did so quite recently. He is still teaching young soldiers to fly helicopters. It's the keen edge of danger in army life that he likes. So he says.

In the end I completed the course in a reasonable time with reasonable results. Nothing special. But at least I hadn't been chopped. A good forty per cent had. The funny thing was that I wouldn't have minded so very much if I had. As far as I was concerned, not getting a chance to fly Beavers seemed to have torpedoed my personal reason for wanting to fly. But I made it, so on I went.

After the ceremonial 'wings' parade and formal 'passing out' there were a number of postings I could go for. I particularly wanted one in the UK, as I had just got engaged to a girl from my home town in Kent.

I was just twenty, the youngest pilot in the three services. Of only two UK possibilities, one was to fly for the Parachute Regiment, the toughest outfit in the army.

My Army Air Corps colleagues warned me off. 'You'll never get out alive,' they said. But I was afraid of nothing. So, in the end, that was the job I got.

A few weeks later I reported for duty at Aldershot, then Brigade HQ. The Brigadier himself welcomed me to the Brigade.

'As far as we're concerned, Marfleet, you're a flying "penguin". *Real* paras have to *earn* their red berets. You get one free. But I need a pilot, so I've got to take you, but I don't have to like it. And what's all this nonsense about getting married? You should be sorting out your career, not setting up home. I suggest you forget it!'

I realized their reputation had not been understated.

As the sun lifted into the crook of the distant mountain range, the valley regained its normal colour, the blues of the morning changing to the verdant green of the jungle, and the rich brown dusty soil of the clearings and ridges. The tribesmen made their way down their side of the valley, and across to the chosen meeting place.

The battlefield was on a dun-coloured clearing half-way up the opposite side of the valley. Here the two tribes met. The warriors who were not fighting, and the women, looked on from high ground or stayed behind by their huts. The reserve force was put into the field but was to take no part, except to recover the injured, or stand in if the front line began to look deeply threatened.

The men had now re-applied their pigs' fat coating, this time mixed with charcoal and ash from the fire to produce striking wavy lines on their faces and bodies. All wore their best gourds. Each carried a bow and flightless arrows, several light throwing spears and their individual stabbing spear. There was no attempt at camouflage or concealment. This was not a raid. This was formal battle.

Moondi's tribe, led by his father, advanced upwards in a ragged line towards the higher jungle boundary of their agreed engagement area. As expected, the enemy had prepared an ambush from the treeline over to the right of the field but, obeying the unwritten rules, had revealed themselves in good time for Moondi's force to be prepared. The fight opened with a rain of arrows in both directions, and developed as the warriors danced and mouthed and chanted, dodging and weaving towards each other, constantly stringing arrows to bows, and occasionally making sallies forward to loose a cast of spears.

The sun lifted high overhead as the two groups of warriors ebbed and flowed over the small area of brown earth. Arrows found their mark, bringing flesh wounds to both sides; throwing spears did more serious damage, and the Spirit Talkers were busily employed in helping the wounded by forcing them to kneel, bending forward, as the Talkers jerked and massaged their falling spirits back up into their chests again.

Some of the fallen warriors would rise, and make their way back down to the shelter of the trees to summon strength for the walk home. But others simply grunted and fell over, fainting, blood streaming from their bodies. Then a pallet was called for, and the patient carried, face down, back to his home. None complained of pain. To be wounded was the lot of a warrior.

Moondi had been in the front line from the beginning, standing close to, and learning from, his father. He began to see how to watch for the arrows and spears, to catch the motion out of the corner of his eye, sight the missile, and leap clear as it landed. He saw how his father had perfected a smooth way of stringing and firing quickly to give the enemy less opportunity to dodge. Arrows from his bow thudded home in arms and legs quite frequently. Those from Moondi's were loosed with less effect. At one point he had led three of his cousins forward in a dash to throw spears. But they were all inexperienced, and the spears were thrown at some risk to themselves—his closest cousin had received an arrow in his foot—but without visible effect on the enemy. In fact, he began to feel the day had gone against them. They had certainly lost more warriors through wounds, though with the continual motion of the line this was hard to detect.

Then Moondi saw his opportunity. Three of the enemy had slipped into a cleft which led directly towards the bottom of the valley. They were, in effect, moving softly around his tribe's flanks. Moondi could see that a flight of arrows from that quarter could deeply upset the course of the fight. But he said nothing, and continued shouting and dancing and loosing arrows as he moved slowly and inconspicuously across to the left of his line.

Suddenly he shouted out, and with a wild over-arm motion pointed at the cleft. Turning, the warriors near him saw their game, and peeled off from the line, swooping down to the ditch on top of the three enemy who were in the act of stringing their first arrows. Moondi's men poured into the cleft firing and throwing, Moondi himself in front shouting and calling out the name of his grandfather. A bow twanged beneath him, and he felt the sharp stab of an arrow in his upraised forearm.

The enemy warrior who had fired turned and desperately scrabbled at the opposite side of the cleft, trying to climb out. Moondi lunged with his stabbing spear. It bit into the back of the retreating tribesman. He gurgled and flailed wildly, and sank into the bottom of the pit in a death agony. In seconds, three warriors lay dead in a bloody pool in the bottom of the ditch.

Moondi roared at his men to disengage, knowing that what had proved a trap for the enemy could as easily prove one for his men too. They responded quickly, and jumped back out of the cleft, running back down the ragged enemy line loosing off arrows as they went. The enemy surged forward, and Moondi called for the warriors to fall back, shouting to his father, 'I have killed, I have killed!'

The line retreated and re-formed at the jungle edge, at

the base of the battlefield. They knew what would happen now. The advancing enemy line reached the cleft, and saw the three dead warriors. They paused, and a low wail emerged from the throats of the motionless tribesmen. Instantly, they turned about and melted into the higher jungle. Moments later, another group came forward and disappeared down into the cleft, re-appearing with the three corpses borne between them. They too turned and trod slowly back into the jungle. The battle was over.

Victory had been ceded to Moondi's tribe. Death and disease would be lifted. But it had been a battle with a sudden and bitter end, and Moondi knew one day the enemy would return to seek vengeance. But for the present he was content. His father had been right. His grandfather's spirit had honoured the choice of battle-field. Proudly Moondi lifted his blood-stained spear, and strode out of the clearing. He paused briefly to snap off the shaft of the arrow embedded in his upper arm against a tree. He ignored the stab of pain and the rivulet of blood. He pushed aside the bobbing, bustling Spirit Talker who intercepted him. What need had he of him? His spirit was swelling manfully in his breast.

He walked on down the base of the valley, and then upward to his walled home. His wife would now be restored by the victory. He badly wanted to see her. He pushed into his garden, and a line of village women blocked his way. Suddenly alarmed, he forced through them and into the darkened doorway of his home. Lanya was lying on her pallet surrounded by her female relatives. They were keening and massaging fire ash into her belly.

'No!' He screamed. 'I have killed! The blood of three warriors is on my head. It *is* enough!' His wife's cold face offered no reply or comfort. Her eyes were open but unsighted. Her body lay quiet. She was dead.

As he stood there, swaying with shock, he heard a sound which he had never heard before. It was like the continuous beating of a small drum, superhumanly fast and without changing rhythm. He fell on to his knees, and put his head on Lanya's belly where her spirit had been. It was cold. He kissed it. Some of the women left and went outside to see what the noise was. The sound was getting louder. There were shouts and cries. Moondi ignored them. He didn't move. He couldn't. He was exhausted, from fighting, from loss of blood, from rent emotions. From everything.

The sound was loud now, beating right over the hut, drowning out the excited and fearful shrieks of the women. It rained down on him through the straw roofing of the dwelling. And somehow, as he lay there weeping on his wife's cold body, not knowing what the new noise was—physical or spiritual, boding good or evil—it seemed to him that the sound of it penetrated his whole being, as though he lay completely at the mercy of it. And yet he was conscious it took no advantage. He was not afraid, but uncannily reassured. It seemed to surround him as he lay. In his overwrought and exhausted state he felt as though the whole destiny of his tribe was linked, through him, to this pounding, relentless noise.

Then, as quickly as it had come, the drumming sound diminished, dropping quickly to the buzzing of an angry bee. Darkness crowded in on him again, and the agony of loss re-established itself. He held Lanya to himself. The women returned chattering and speculating about what they had heard and seen. They fell silent when they saw him, and remembered the dead. They picked up their keening chant again, and gathered around him, touching his back gently with their broken hands.

At the head of the valley, between the crook of the hills, the declining sun glinted momentarily off the polished wings of a departing aeroplane.

5

Foreign Fields

In fact I explained to the brigadier that getting married was more sensible than my shooting off back to Tonbridge at all hours. Best to have the girl of my dreams here on the patch so to speak. He saw my point. Either way it didn't matter a great deal to him—for my para detachment was off overseas. So I packed my bags, kissed my new wife Mary goodbye, and joined my new Sioux, minus rotor head, inside an RAF Hercules transport aircraft bound for Cyprus. Bright-eyed and bushy tailed.

One thing bothered me a bit. As the brigadier had said, I wasn't really a para. Although I was required to wear the distinctive red beret, that was a kind of courtesy. I continued to wear the Army Air Corps badge on it. Flying taxi driver to the regiment I was. Someone to scout out ahead, or pull them out of trouble. That was fine. A beret I was allowed. But no para wings to supplement it. They were reserved for the Real Thing. Yet in command and control situations, the paras would be expected to do what I, as an infantry officer, said. They didn't like that. Frankly, neither did I. But I was flying for them so I'd fly like a para. I'd show them.

The overseas tour looked interesting enough. It was only for a matter of weeks—hence the UK 'base'—but, being newly married, it was not much fun. Nobody deserves to be left alone in Aldershot. And Mary least of all. I concentrated on the future.

First, the Parachute Regiment Gunners (7th Parachute Regiment Royal Horse Artillery, and-don't-you-forget-it) were to practise lobbing shells up country, quartered in Dekelia, the second British Sovereign base. I was to intersperse this with patrols up in the Cypriot highlands—chasing up bandits who had a penchant for losing themselves in the mountains—and then follow that with a trip to Ethiopia. Sounded good to me. I told Mary it was important experience. I would be facing all manner of strange and challenging flying conditions. And, though I didn't know it, facing all manner of strange and challenging creatures. Not all of them paras. She sighed, and prepared for more evenings alone in Aldershot.

Cyprus was warm and welcoming, and I settled enthusiastically into the role of pilot to the paras. Gunnery came first. And for me nearly last. I was just about to switch off when a voice buzzed in my helmet on the gunnery radio net.

'Hello, One Five. This is Range I/G. Over.'

'Range I/G, this is One Five. Go ahead.'

'One Five, we have stores for one more shoot. Over.'

'One Five, roger. I'm on my way. Out.'

I was sitting inside my Sioux on the landing field at Dekelia feeling pretty pleased with myself. My machine was still warm after a hard morning's ranging for the guns of the Troop. This, a hark back to the very first work for aircraft in the army, was still a vital job. I had learned to fly up high, and spot targets out of the line of sight of the battery which was firing—and they would lay their guns totally on my reports and corrections. And it had worked pretty well. The morning had passed, we had hit some targets and missed others, but over all I was pleased. I could handle this. A whole battery of guns banging away at my direction, blowing big holes in the distant countryside. Powerful stuff. From 2,000 feet I had magnanimously congratulated them on their efforts, and they had returned the compliment. I was thinking about an lunch when the Instructor of Gunnery—Captain George St John-Mountgay (you could tell he was from the RHA just by the name)—called up for one more go.

So I lit up and lit out. One minute thirty seconds later I was back on the ground thanking the Lord for Sergeant Farmer and his engine-off landing drills. Mine had just quit on me. A cough and then nothing. I was fortunate to have had enough height to make it in at all. Shaking with sudden shock I called base, and the Flight Commander came whistling out in his Landrover.

'What happened, David?' he quizzed. I explained as well as I could.

'Not touched anything?' I said that I hadn't. After any accident it's pretty important not to. I knew that. It's like evidence at the scene of a crime. The smallest thing might give a clue. And save others' lives.

He checked around the cockpit. And straightened up. 'Sure, David?' In a sort of relieved but where-on-earth-do-they-*find*-these-new-pilots-nowadays kind of voice.

'Yes, sir.'

'The fuel is switched off, David.' I looked at him, thunderstruck.

'Well, see for yourself.'

I looked. It was. I must have got airborne on what was left in the carburettor! Dumbfounded, I thought back to what I had done. On shutting down, I had turned it off. Then, still sitting in the aircraft, the call had come in from the range, and I had started up right away. But how had I missed turning it on? Light dawned. Normally, the fuel was turned on when a pilot was doing his external walk around—the pre-flight check. Remember the bit with the penny and the tail rotor? At that stage you leant into the cockpit, and pushed the knob *in* to turn the fuel *on* from *outside*. I had never actually got out, and so missed the normal, familiar, sequence.

Drinks on me that night in the mess. And one early note in the flying experience column. For the next few weeks, I tell you, I checked 'fuel on' every ten minutes—wherever I was.

But the tone for the tour was set when, pulling off a high mountain top one fresh morning, I was spilling down the side of a precipice when something moved *behind* the instrument panel. Now, in the Sioux there isn't much of an instrument panel anyway, and what there is doesn't contain anything which might conceivably move. No mechanics, no pressure valves, nothing. As I was diving fast, I concentrated for a moment on the flying. The air was thin at that height so I had to keep moving forward or fall out of the sky.

A helicopter usually flies with a mixture of forward movement and vertical lift from the rotor blades. Unless the engine is very powerful, it can usually only 'hang on the blades'—or hover—at low altitudes where the air is thicker, and they can get a good 'bite'. For the Sioux, notoriously underpowered, that was below 4,000 feet. Anywhere above, and I had to keep moving. The altimeter needle was falling past 7,000 feet when the bottom of the panel moved again. I leant forward. Looking back at me were two fixed beady eyes, a delicate nose and a flickering forked tongue. I was not alone. There was a snake under the instruments.

Now, I know James Bond tends to handle this kind of problem all the time as part of his service career, but I have certainly never claimed to be in his league. Not when it comes to handling snakes, anyway.

The mountains and valleys slid past automatically as I watched the thing slowly coil its way hopefully up my rudder pedals. The movement was arousing his interest. I knew I couldn't land. At this altitude the speed I needed to fly meant I would smash into the ground and break up if I even tried. I thought of my trusty service revolver or, to be strictly accurate, my 9 mm automatic pistol strapped to my thigh. I had seen a few westerns in my time. But the idea of controlling a skeetering helicopter, in mountains, while coolly and deliberately shooting my instrument panel and plexiglass canopy to pieces in the hope that I might hit a snake, seemed to me to be roughly in the same book as a crash landing.

The sinuous beast was making loving moves towards my flying boots when my hand, feeling around the seat for something to poke with, grasped the handle of the portable fire extinguisher. Holding the collective lever in place with the pressure of my knee (important when you need a spare hand) I wrenched the extinguisher free.

'TOXIC FUMES. NOT TO BE USED IN A CONFINED SPACE' it said on it in big red letters. I banged the release button. An acrid blast of fire-fighting gas and liquid jetted into the cockpit hitting the snake between the eyes, knocking it back behind the instrument panel. Chemical frost bloomed over the plexiglass canopy. But I wasn't looking. Like the engine driver of the 6-5 Special, I was hanging out of the door in the roar of the slip-stream, blades whipping overhead, poisonous fumes pouring out around me, with only two fingers stretched out on the cyclic, flying by the seat of my pants.

RAF Akrotiri rose up ahead, and I called for landing. The controller was possibly a little concerned to see me arrive in a puff of smoke looking like Casey Jones on holiday. But he had seen a lot of things in his time, especially new army pilots, and since I hadn't declared an emergency he made no comment. Most of the fumes had gone by then, anyway.

As soon as the skids touched concrete I sweated the regulation two minutes run down before clearing the side. Nothing seemed to be moving down by my boots. The machine wound down slowly in the warm sun. Sweat steamed vigourously off my flying suit. Cicadas chirruped nonchalantly in the undergrowth, and from the hangar came the comforting hammering of an aircraft engineer addressing his trade. A quiet morning. I walked around to look in the front of the Sioux. Still nothing stirred. Peering inside, I found the snake curled up at the bottom of the cockpit, its fire out for good. Gingerly I removed the limp remains.

'Where d'you get that, sir?' asked one of the aircraft handlers as he fitted the parking wheels to the skids preparatory to walking the machine back into the hangar. I told him.

'Aw, sir, you don't want to worry about *them*, sir. They're harmless. Get loads of 'em around here, we do.'

'Thank you, Wilmot,' I said evenly. 'I'll try to remember that.'

Altitude and animals did not seem to mix well for me in the early days. Shortly after the snake incident, I was required to assist the police in their patrols on the hills. We had a dog contingent, and they were much valued as bandit hunters. But, because there were few of them, we flew them to the spot when called out by the regular police or troops. Again the altitude caused problems. Up above 4,000 feet I had to keep moving to keep airborne. Not very fast, unless I was really high, but I had to keep going. This was no real problem to either the dog-handlers or the dogs who could both individually judge the jump out—rather like getting off a fast-moving escalator. The problem came when they had to do it together. Somehow they always got fouled up, and I would end up swirling off in a cloud of dust with handler and dog piled up in a tangled heap below.

They came up with a solution. An external kennel. Mounted out on the skids, this was expressly designed so that when the handler pulled a line from the cockpit the flap at the front would open, and the dog, having had some training to that effect, would leap out. Thus, they could time it exactly. It worked well. That is until one day I was up at 5,000 feet, the catch came loose and the door fell open ... and ... you can guess the rest. I landed back at

Akrotiri with the handler whimpering like a baby and no dog. Later the patrols did carry on. But the kennel had a double safety lock fitted. You learn by your mistakes in the air. Usually the hard way.

That tour, the animal kingdom was determined to leave its impression on me. From the mountains of Cyprus I was sent to the desert heartland of Ethiopia. A vast country with mile after mile of open scrubby countryside. Of course it has cultivated areas, but not where we were.

Our task was to build a bridge. Several, in fact. This was to be accomplished by a smart team of Royal Engineers operating on loan to the Ethiopian government. Only the UK had not quite got a clear message about what was wanted. UK Land Forces HQ, that is. Word came through from the Foreign Office: 'Send engineers. We're going to make a bridge.' And UKLF easily converted this into: 'Send engineers. We've got to clear a ridge,' or something similar. The result was the RE team I found when I flew out were all bulldozer experts, minus bulldozers.

'Bridge? What bridge? Don't know nothing about a bridge. Do you know anything about a bridge, Sarge?'

Now, though I say it myself, it turned out that the helicopter pilot was the best qualified bridge-builder of the lot. Remember Sapper Marfleet?

In the end, we got all the bridges up and the roads open ahead of time and, not being one to hang around when there was trouble to get into, I persuaded some of the dafter Sappers to join me in an ecologically meaningful crocodile count down the Blue Nile. The only vessel to hand for the voyage was the army standard assault inflatable. An *inflatable* for a crocodile count? Well, it looked fine to me, so four of us embarked for the trip.

We soon found ourselves paddling away downstream, and counting for all we were worth. What I hadn't realized—which was important both for my statistics and my health—was that crocs can lie just *under* the surface as well as up on top. In fact, it is much their favourite style. We soon came across just such a one. To say it was annoyed would have been an understatement. It reared up in front of us, jaws snapping and tail thrashing. Jagged teeth ripped through the flimsy rubber of our buoyancy tubes, and the inflatable bubbled across the river exhaling like a spent balloon. I have never seen Sappers move so fast in my life. In our fast deflating craft we paddled furiously for a sandbank. I had taken a rifle with me for safety, and I was tempted during the fracas to take a shot at the croc. I'm glad I didn't. I was told later that unless properly aimed, bullets tend to bounce off. The crocs just get more irritated. This one was irritated enough, but must have eaten by then, or thought us indigestible, as thankfully he left us alone with our struggles.

We got to the sand bar, and surveyed the damage. Assault inflatables are supposed to be built like ships—in watertight, buoyant compartments. Hole one and others carry on. Buoyantly. Ours was more like the Titantic: the compartments were there but the buoyancy wasn't. We sat warily on the sand, and debated the issue. Eventually, we decided to patch up what we could and re-launch. We were more than a hundred miles from civilization so we didn't have much choice. For the rest of the trip we took turns on the air pump, squeezing away the miles, putting back in what pressure the tooth holes let out. In the end, progress being slow in the damaged craft, we were picked up as we neared home—by a search party who had set out when we became overdue. We said we hadn't counted many crocodiles, having found ourselves engaged in more animate research.

At the end of our stay there was a guard of honour, and dinner with Emperor Haile Selassie in his palace—a kind of thank you for the bridges—and some of us got a medal for services rendered to Ethiopia. We were welcome back any time, he said, but told us to remember the crocodiles were quieter in the rainy season.

If Ethiopia was scrubby desert, I got the real thing in Arabia, dunes and all. The United Arab Emirates, old friends of Britain, had been having trouble with the Yemen shortly after our withdrawal from Aden, and a deal was struck for the SAS to help out with border patrols, and generally assist in deterring the (then) Communist-backed Yemenis from encroaching on to UAE territory. The SAS were there only in very small groups, but were professional in the extreme, both in their soldiering and their attitude. I was hugely impressed. Many of them had come from the paras, but there were Guards and many other top units represented, and they worked together in tight, informal teams, living out in the desert. Later I was to get to know the SAS better, but this was an impressive introduction. Keen soldiers, tough, independent and courageous. They were the very cream of the army.

My job was re-supply. I had to fly out to a map reference in the desert (not dreadfully helpful—it's just sand. Often I was just given a compass-bearing and distance out) to drop off food and equipment. Having made sure the SAS were there, of course. I didn't always see them. But they would see me—and tell me where to drop. Then I'd fly back to base to do the same thing five days or a week later, often many miles away from where they had been before. On one day it would be high in the border mountains, another in the wide open sea of the desert. Often if they were 'out on ops' I would land and have a chat with them, chew the fat, pass on the news and gossip from the base, and tell them what was happening in the world—that kind of thing.

Desert flying itself was odd. Especially at night. Once clear of the coast there are no ground lights whatsoever. Often it is overcast, so there are no stars or moon. No external references at all. Then a strange feeling creeps over you. You suddenly feel you are floating, quite still, in a giant goldfish bowl. Nothing is moving. You are suspended, hanging there in space. Known as vertigo, it is an impression which is very dangerous to pilots—for obvious reasons—and something which the aviation doctors began to look into very seriously around this time.

The Sioux was bad for this in one respect: the bubble canopy gave you the goldfish effect without really trying. The only way to overcome the feeling was to force yourself to wobble the stick, lock your eyes on to the instruments, and force yourself to believe them. Alternatively, you could stick your head out into the slip-stream, and get a faceful of seventy-knot air. You knew you were moving then. The Scout, a helicopter I was to transfer on to later, was much worse according to the reports although it had no bubble canopy. No one could work out why. Scout pilots were reporting that they had believed they were sitting out the back on the tail, or on top of the rotor head. Very strange.

Once in this sort of state it was very difficult to recover. The procedure was to press your hands sharply together and waggle the stick. If you then felt in control, fine. Don't worry about where you think you are. You can fly the aircraft sitting on the tail if need be. Then check your instruments, noting the readings individually (normally pilots are taught to scan quickly from one to another). 120 knots. *Mmm, must be going fast, that's all right then.* 2,000 feet. *Mmm, fancy that. Must be above the ground then. Let's keep it that way.* And so on.

This ridiculous procedure actually worked, and saved a number of lives. They discovered why it particularly affected the Scout in the end. It was the navy who came up with the answer. They were busy deploying a similar helicopter known as the Wasp on their frigates, and so getting a lot of information about how it performed in low reference environments over water. It seemed that the tail navigation light was being turned into a strobe through the rotor blades, and this was being reflected down into the corner of the pilot's eye by a white check-list mounted over the windscreen. At night, the effect sent him into something like a cataleptic trance. After that discovery, the check-list was re-sited lower down the windscreen, and the problem—in this unique form—went away. I never really faced it seriously myself, even in the Sioux. But then most people said I hadn't enough imagination to see myself as a pilot, let alone a goldfish.

Towards the end of my time in the United Arab Emirates I was on SAS call again, but I just couldn't locate them. They were in the foothills near the border. I tracked up and down, calling all the while for landmarks which the lost patrol endeavoured to give me. No use. Not a hide nor hair could I find. And they were out in the open. Fuel started to get low so, reluctantly, I came on net and announced no show. I promised to come out again the next day. A plaintive voice buzzed back.

'You can't just *go*. We haven't eaten for three days!'

'OK,' I said. 'I know what. You make some smoke. Just light up anything that comes to hand.'

Very shortly, at about nine o'clock, I saw a thin wisp low on the horizon. In two minutes I was blowing up a sandstorm around a group of nomadic desert goatherds who were also British Special Forces. Their mess tins were almost clanking with anticipation as I pulled the ration packs out of the Sioux. I joined them for a cuppa around their fire. I saw one of them had slung a copper wire over a gorse bush, and was tapping away on a Morse key. Intrigued, I asked who he was talking to. 'Hereford,' was the monosyllabic reply.

Hereford was the SAS headquarters in England. I laughed. Back on the coast the Royal Signals had spent weeks trying to get a decent signal back to the UK. We'd flown out experts, who'd calculated skip distances, drawn attenuation diagrams, discussed skywave interference patterns, not to mention altering the orientation of a forest of radio aerials by tiny fractions of a degree. They had allowed for almost everything except the colour of the signalman's pyjamas. And we still had problems getting through. Here was a tiny patrol in the desert chattering away to base with a wire slung over a gorse bush. It's the way they train them, these SAS.

But, back on the coast, signals were getting through. And one had my name on it. Sun, sand and soft skies were over. My time had come.

It was my turn for Northern Ireland.

6

Indian Country

Four days at home in Mary's loving arms, and I was off. That was the rub.

'Oh, David,' she wondered sadly one morning, 'I thought a UK posting meant we would be together.'

'Me too, darling. But I don't think we quite reckoned with the army.' We hadn't. In fact, in the four years I spent 'UK-based', I spent less than twelve months working from home. Air-mobile meant what it said. This time, though, there was an edge to the parting. In addition to the hazards of the air, I was to face those from the ground as well. I had more experience, it was true. But not under fire.

I was greeted on the first day by the 'Northern Ireland Orientation Briefing'. It was sobering stuff.

'Remember,' said the major of intelligence leaning his large bulk, the product of years of desk-top soldiering, cautiously against the lectern, 'the terrorist always has the upper hand. You don't know who he—or she—is. Could be the milkman, could be the dustman, the petrol pump attendant, shop assistant, anyone at all. You don't know when they are going to strike or where. But,' here he paused significantly, '*they* all know who *you* are. And *where* you are and, most likely, when you are going to be back—so they can get a little surprise ready for you. It's all very one-sided. It's dirty. It's unpleasant, and it's wasteful. But it's the job we've got. So watch your backs, and trust *no one*.'

All the same, I thought, as I sped out over the rolling countryside in my green-painted Sioux with ARMY picked out in ten-inch high white letters on the side of my fuel tanks, at least the infantry had the odd ditch to drop into if things got warm. Up here there weren't too many places to hide. And as for the plexiglass . . . I felt just a little exposed, sitting there floating above the peat bogs in a plastic goldfish bowl. All that wonderful visibility seemed suddenly on the generous side.

I had been issued with the personal Macrilon body armour recommended for pilots. But, as did the other pilots, I felt it left a lot to be desired. Looking like Michelin Man may make you feel secure, but if you can't drive the helicopter . . . We plumped for the much lighter, though less defensive, flak jacket as a compromise. At least you could fly in it.

And fly I did. It was a busy time. Like everyone who has not visited the Province, I had gained the impression that there would be snipers under every bush, and there weren't. But in a sense this was the danger. A week or two would go by without an incident—then wham! Something miserable would hit you. And the headlines.

To start with, new pilots were introduced to the operational routines and routes by doing the mail-drops. Each defended position and troop centre—be it RUC police station or local barracks, school house, defended farm or country house—had a mail-drop. Nothing moved by road if it could be moved by air. And mail could be moved by air.

Every day I and my Sioux would do the rounds. Each route had a name: Carnaby Street, Oxford Street, Mayfair, and so on. And you followed it. Religiously. The names never changed, and there were only so many routes. Why the hoods didn't just lie in wait and open fire on arrival I'll never know. But they didn't. Not then.

I had a scare one morning, though. I was just dropping

in over the roof-tops to a battalion HQ in Dungannon when I spotted someone on a chimney-pot lifting out a long dark item. The blades fairly crackled as I fed in the power and performed a wall of death turn out of his line of fire. Nothing happened. So I took a closer look. The long dark item had by now been joined by another. With a round spiky head on it. It was the local chimney-sweep finishing off the job up top! I came in, and landed bumpily on the helipad. I don't know who was vibrating the most—me or the Sioux.

Graduating from mail-drops, I found there was actually one worse 'sitting duck' duty. These were the 'culvert patrols'. Not covert . . . culvert. The requirement was to fly down beside the roads where an army convoy was due, and check *underneath* that no one had put any nasties down. The roads were criss-crossed with drainage culverts which could conceal quite effectively hundreds of pounds of explosive. In the early days the mix was highly nitrogenous fertilizer and kerosene. Add a fistful of plastic explosive and a detonator, and you had your bomb. It was horribly effective, and we lost many good men that way. So the short answer was to send us out at hover-mower height looking up drains for the land-mines.

The weakness of the argument from our pilot's perspective was that if you had planted something in a culvert the chances were you'd be watching it, and if a nice army helicopter came snooping about you'd as likely let him have it, or at least a couple of rounds from the Kalashnikov, as the intended target. But we did it, nevertheless.

But if the drains were a pain, 'comms link' was truly riveting. Because the British army at the time had mostly field radios and nothing else, communication between patrols on the streets was non-existent. Only with a helicopter aloft could anybody talk to anybody else. So I and my aerial colleagues would be up there all hours passing on confidential messages like a waiter in a singles restaurant.

A street patrol would call me on station:

'Hello, Army One Five. This is Ranger Eight Eight. Over.'

'Ranger Eight Eight, this is One Five. Go ahead.'

'One Five, this is Eight Eight. Have turned corner of Street Six Seven Bravo. Recce code: Zero. Over.'

'Eight Eight, this is One Five. Roger. Will pass your message. Out.'

Then I would call brigade HQ:

'Ranger Control, this is Army One Five.'

'Yes, Army One Five, this is Ranger Control. Over.'

'Ranger Eight Eight reports corner of Fazackerly Street. Nothing seen. Over.'

'Ranger Control. Roger. Out.'

Now this is not exactly crackling stuff, and after an hour or so you felt you wanted to make like a para, and jump out just to improve on the interest. Every message from foot patrol to base and back again was relayed, by voice, through the helicopter. In the end we introduced a 'brevity code'—just call-sign and numbers to indicate specific messages. But that too had its drawbacks. Get one number wrong, and you had the whole patrol pinned down under mortar fire rather than breaking off for a quick cuppa. Then the list of things you could convey with numbers got so long it was quicker to say it all than look it up in the latest directory-sized 'brevity' code book. It was a good thing when they all got UHF radios like the police.

Some nights, though, I *was* able to help out. One evening a unit from the Light Infantry reported taking fire. I copied this through to HQ who quickly whistled up some reinforcements. Then I flew over to take a look. I could see the muzzle flashes of automatic weapons sparkling back and forth below me in the darkness. And, as I watched, a funny thought occurred to me: I knew Belfast Military District was divided up into two brigade groups, and the Light Infantry squawk had been sent from pretty close to their brigade group boundary. I quickly re-tuned my radio, the standard mobile ARC44, to the adjacent 39 Brigade's calling frequency—I with my airborne set being the only one who could listen to both—and just caught the close of a call from a marine of 45 Commando shouting that he too was in a fire-fight. Marine reinforcements were hitting the streets even as he spoke. I took another look down at the the muzzle flashes, and at my A-Z street plan of Belfast. I was sure of it. They were shooting at each other!

Back I went on the net, this time with some urgency. But no one was listening! They were having such a wonderful time blazing away at each other in the darkness. I started using voice procedure that was certainly not in the communications manual. Eventually my bad manners, and a blanket refusal to pass any more messages until both parties exchanged map references, called a halt.

Suddenly the street went quiet. The reinforcements slipped quietly back to barracks. When they checked up they found they had been firing at each other for over twenty minutes. It was fortunate no one was hurt.

Aldergrove Airport, on the banks of Lough Neigh, was base for 664 Para Squadron Army Air Corps. We lived in the military police mess there. Alan Stirling was a rangy and provocative type. He had been newly promoted from Warrant Officer. And Dave Witney and Dave Rowat were older sergeant pilots who gave me a lot of help on my first tour. In one way, it was a good thing that I was a penguin. The two Daves could legitimately look upon me as a jumped-up sub-standard rookie—and so take a lot of trouble to make sure I knew what I was about before I was let loose. They took a lot of care.

I found that paras basically come in two editions: short and taut, or wide and weighty. Dave Rowat was of the former type: an all-macho man, bags-of-smoke-over-the-top type. Good soldier and good pilot to have around. Dave Witney was even tougher, and a keen 'jumper' —

having been in the Red Devils free-fall team, and Alan, like me, was just, well, a penguin. Both of us learned to feel inferior together.

In fact, Dave Witney saved my life that first tour just by being a sergeant. A patrol was called, and my number was in the frame. I was about to leave for dispersal when Dave put his head around the door, and asked if I'd mind if he did this one—and take the evening off. Straight swap. I couldn't see a problem. Evenings were no riot for me anyway, since I was separated from Mary by the Irish Sea.

He took off and, over an open piece of country half-way down 'Carnaby Street', the turbo-charger blew, and his engine lost interest. Smoothly he put into effect all the hours of 'engine-off' training that his instructor had no doubt given him, and put the Sioux down in a convenient field next to the road. That was a mistake. Not, under the circumstances, something that he could have avoided. But because the road was so close it led others to make a fateful decision.

Dave's first feeling on getting down was not so much relief as fear. Following an emergency landing most pilots are so grateful to be safe on the ground that they consider it their right to relax the tensions of the day with a cigarette or similar until the rescue boys turn up. But Indian country, as he told me later, is different. In Indian country, the main problem is staying alive *after* you have landed. In Northern Ireland no soldier is safe. Especially on his own, and having advertised his arrival in such a spectacular manner.

He knew he had to get out. Immediately. Aldergrove had answered his 'Mayday' so there was nothing to keep him. Drawing his pistol, Dave scuttled out of his machine like it was already taking hits, and fled across the open field looking for concealment, noting en route that his pistol did not quite have the range or stopping power of a Kalashnikov. He found a ditch at the end. He jumped in smartly, pulling weeds and mud around him, and did his best to pretend he was a water-rat with two beady eyes and the muzzle of his pistol peeping out of the undergrowth. There he stayed until the Landrover patrol arrived, and a platoon secured the area.

It was then the decision was taken: the Sioux would be recovered by road. Out came the transporter, and Dave stood by to supervise the hoisting of the machine on to the flatbed. Several hours later, the convoy was ready to depart. Dave banged the truck driver on the shoulder, and ran back to the leading Landrover, hopped in the back and wedged himself on to the floor. As an afterthought he slung his flak jacket over his head. He was wet and tired, and would get in a few 'zeds' before arrival back at Aldergrove.

They blew the Landrover off the road. Curled up, underneath the flak jacket, Dave survived. Just. He woke up in hospital. I said his being a sergeant saved me. No, swopping the duty had done that. Being a sergeant saved him. If I had been there, as an officer I would have been expected to sit in the front of the Landrover. The driver, front passenger and two soldiers all died. After that, downed helicopters were recovered by air, and both he and I always flew with a sub-machine-gun tucked under our seats, and a couple of magazines on the side, in addition to our pistols.

Slowly, with my comrades' help, I was becoming what the army wanted: a pilot and a soldier. I was building up my flying skills and my military confidence. I was very shortly to need both. I had moved on to the 'command and control' stage now. This usually meant giving a leg-weary infantry major a ride while his 'toms' did the patrol on foot.

One day, I was over Armagh, and had on board a major from the Gordon Highlanders. He was known as something of a wild card. Something to do with Scottish ancestry I expect. We were windmilling gently over the outskirts of Armagh when the radio sizzled to life bearing the unmistakable accent of the regimental sergeant major of the Gordons.

'Och, Army Airborne, are ye no' there?'

'Army One Five. How can I help. Over?'

'Some o' the boys come in a wee bit of bother in the Craigellan Estate, sirrah. Can ye no do som'at for them?'

'One Five. Roger. Wilco.' Prompt Battle of Britain style always impresses when help is required.

'Och, and have ye seen any of wee Major McNulty aboot at all, sirrah? I canna raise him.'

'Major McNulty is with me. Over.'

There was a regimental clearing of the throat.

'Och! Could ye tell the major, sirrah: the colonel wants him to see the boys oot of there anywa' ye can. Out.'

I hauled the machine around, and spun over Armagh to recce the problem. Major McNulty traced the area on his Ordnance Survey map. Flyover, road, built-up area, estate. All Indian country. Foot patrol probably surprised at a street crossing, I surmised. Then we saw them. At the same time they dialled up the back pack frequency, and came up on the Sioux's net. Their sergeant spoke. They had been caught by a 'come on' he informed me amid the background atmospheric 'ping' of ricocheting rifle rounds. They had been inspecting a stolen car when they had come under fire from at least two buildings on the estate. Ordinarily they would have withdrawn the way they had come. But their escape was now blocked by a group of rioters marching on the flyover who were ripping up paving-stones, and dropping them on to the road below. Scots or no they would have needed more than their steel helmets to run the gauntlet of that lot.

Pinned down was right. And I couldn't see a way out, barring calling up an all-out assault. And by the time that could be organized they would have taken casualties. I couldn't lift them out, and as for us flushing out the snipers ourselves—well, two pistols between us, and several layers of tiling and plaster over them (they were firing from buildings) ruled out that one. Somehow I had to draw the rioters off. Major McNulty was equal to the occasion.

'We'll boomb the boog'rs,' he opined, pulling out two CS gas canisters which he had artfully concealed about his person. 'I kenned they'd come in handy one o' these fine days,' he reflected.

'Ah, right.'

I could see what he had in mind. The CS would disperse the rioters long enough for the trapped Gordons to make a dash for freedom. It could work . . . as long as no one saw us coming. That, I figured, would be up to me.

I made the Jocks party to the plan. They were delighted to hear we had a scheme, but were unhappy about one detail. They didn't have their gas masks with them.

'Well, Sergeant,' I quipped, 'if you don't think you can manage we can always come back tomorrow.'

'Noo, ye dinna want to be doing that, sirrah. Just ye gi'e us the worrd!'

I promised I would. Now for the difficult bit. Major McNulty had already gleefully extracted the safety pins from the gas canisters so I was glad I warned him before my next manoeuvre. A CS charge firing off in the cockpit would have done for the both of us. We didn't have respirators either.

As it was, he clung manfully on to both the Sioux and the canisters, while the twin spires of Armagh Cathedral filled the plexiglass canopy, and swung horizontal as I pulled away from the estate, and plunged in a turning dive towards the deck—collective on the floor, and instruments unwinding like broken watches. Now we were flying.

'Just taking precautions, sir. Keeping low,' I told him. I needn't have worried. He thought it was wonderful, and muted Highland whoops came from the other side of the cockpit as we raced down upon the innocent high-street shoppers below. I hoisted the collective, and gunned the power, winding energy back into the whistling blades which thudded and echoed loudly as we slid below the building line. The street lamps of the high street came level. Too high. I went down some more. Now I was right on top of the cars. Some banged their brakes, others swerved, but my eyes were now on the slip road to the flyover. I could afford to watch nothing else but the flashing street lamps above my head, and the rising parapet of the flyover. I was rocketing straight towards it just as fast and as low as I could go.

'Steady, steady . . . *wires*,' I muttered to myself. 'Watch for *wires*!'

The street seemed clear. I couldn't see any. I thumbed the radio. 'Standby, standby . . .'

The major was by now singing an old Gordon's marching song principally to himself but, as he was now mostly hanging out of the door in the slip-stream, also to most of Armagh. The canisters were clasped close to his chest. He was held in just by his lap strap.

'Hang on, sir!' I bellowed across, in case his enthusiasm for the chase caused him to throw too early.

Suddenly the blue-grey parapet rail of the flyover sprang out of the concrete background as I lined the clattering Sioux up on target. That was my aiming-point.

'Now, now, *now*!' I held the radio button on the stick hard down as I whipped it back into the seat, pulling up power simultaneously with my left hand.

'Go, Jocks, go!' I yelled on the net.

The helicopter reared up over the flyover like a startled horse, and two steel canisters of gas sprang from the major's exaltant grasp, and hit the ground in the midst of the rioters. Stinging smoke streamed out in all directions buffeted by the downwash of my rotors. Instantly the crowd backed away, covering their eyes and mouths with clothes and handkerchiefs, dropping paving-stones and bricks where they stood. Out of the corner of my eye I

saw a platoon of soldiers running flat out for the under-
pass. Heads down, feet pounding.

In a few seconds it was all over. They were through,
and off in their waiting Landrovers. The net crackled,
and a rather wheezy but grateful sergeant came on the
line.

'Greet, One Five. Just greet, sirrah!'

I was pleased.

'Let's get oot o' here, laddie,' broke in the major.
'We're all they've got to shoot at noo!'

Stupidly, I was still circling over the chaos I had
created. I broke left to avoid the vengeance of the
thwarted snipers, pulled some height, and gave ops a
call. The major gave him the good news.

We flew back to Belfast at a sensible height.

'Ah, very much obliged to ye there, Lieutenant.'

'No trouble, sir. Call any time.'

'Yoursel' just come oot with the paras then?' he
quizzed.

Wearing my flying helmet I showed no tell-tale army
beret of identity.

'Yes indeed, sir.'

'Och, I needn't ha' worried mysel' then, need I?' he
grinned. 'You chaps canna stop droppin' in on folk!'

I smiled, accepting the infantry officer's compliment.

It had gone well. I could now say I was an army pilot. It
was just a pity I couldn't say I was a real para.

It was getting to me. Try as I might, I just wasn't part of
the team. When I got back home I had some news for
Mary. Alan Stirling and I had decided to do 'P Company',
the notorious paratroop induction course. Together.

'Well, I suppose if he can do it, then you can, darling,'
she observed drily. 'He smokes over fifty a day, and is
about twice your age.' Which wasn't strictly true. But he
was thirty-six, and he *did* smoke.

'At least you'll be home,' she added. 'In some shape or
other.' She was quite right. In no way was 'P Company'

going to be a picnic. Physically or mentally. And it was going to be Mary who got me through.

7

Para

'Come along, sir. Come along. That lot up there is *winning*, sir. Can't you see that, sir? They're ahead of you, and they're doing better than you—*and you don't seem to mind . . .sir!*'

Friendly Sergeant Lewis of 'P Company' wasn't so far from the truth. I had mainly ceased to mind a good eight miles back. As had most of the rest of my platoon. The only goal now in most of our heads was to make it through. Somehow. Anyhow.

The exercise was one unique to 'P Company'. Called the stretcher race, it was a nine-mile course through the mountains which we had to cover in around two hours, carrying a stretcher loaded with a very uncomfortable spare man.

It was a test of stamina and endurance. The added dimension was that the stretcher forced the dozen in the platoon to work, or rather stagger, together. Four carrying the stretcher, four carrying their rifles (plus their own—and everyone had full packs), and four just running and 'recovering'. The jobs were, of course, rotated. It was also supposed to be a race. Most parts of 'P Company' were a test of physical stamina and endurance. Running up hills, jumping down valleys, assaulting assault courses, surviving survival courses, and forcing forced marches. They told us that we'd never be as fit ever again. 'Fit for what?' we were tempted to ask. But 'P Company' was also about mental stamina. The ability to go on thinking when aching and exhausted. To keep on working—and fighting— under mental pressure. At that moment, Sergeant Lewis was the mental pressure. What he was actually trying to do was needle me into over-stretching myself and the platoon in an attempt to get ahead and win. Over-exhausted we'd perhaps fail to make it at all. He was nice like that.

But we had listened at the briefing. Even, regular pressure. Just keep going. Win through by slogging on steadily. No heroics. Whatever the provocation. And Sergeant Lewis was definitely provocation.

'Don't you *care*, sir? They're just walking away with it. Bit more effort and you'll take them, sir. Easy. Just a bit more...' This approach was something that Alan had responded to magnificently. With the wisdom of his advanced years he had seen through their style on the first day.

'Bunch of wind-up merchants, the lot of them. That's all they are. Psyching you up. Huh, I tell you I'm getting through "P Company" *my* way, not theirs.'

He took out a cigarette, and turned to me. 'Jesus given you any clues on the weather for tomorrow's hike then, David?'

Sometimes I don't know who enjoyed my faith more. Alan or me. But he kept to his adopted style. Up the top of some rain-sodden hillside, below the tree-line, he would suddenly call a halt. His platoon dropping exhausted all around him, he would gently ease a waterproofed packet of cigarettes out of his combat jacket, and light up. The sergeants went pink bananas.

'*Sir*! What *do* you think you are doing, sir? You're on "*P Company*", sir, not a picnic. You *can't* just sit *down*. You'll all lose points if you don't check in on time. Remember that, sir.'

But this and other attempts at corporate blackmail among the platoon just slid off Alan like the rain off his camouflaged Barbour jacket.

'Smoko, Sergeant, smoko. Good for troop morale, etc. You know that. Can't help it if no one else smokes, can I? D'you know I could have sworn Lieutenant Marfleet said it would be fine . . .'

The sergeants soon learned that whatever the delay Alan and his platoon always caught up. No matter how much down time for 'smoko' they took, somehow they made superhuman efforts, and redeemed the situation. It wasn't the normal way, but Alan's individuality gave his platoon character, and they excelled because of it. They finished the course, and earned their berets.

But Alan was the exception. Most of us had as much as we could do just keeping up and slogging on. Mind-numbing exercise followed mind-numbing exercise. Our war cry was always, 'It's only pain!' Or as one course officer put it, 'It's all just mind over matter. I don't mind, and you don't matter!'

For hundreds of miles—literally—we slipped and slid up and down Welsh hills, locating watery map references, making emergency bivouacs without tents or sleeping-bags, cooking over tiny field burners, and trying to stay dry for another twenty-four hours. Surviving. That was it, just surviving. It was murder pure and simple.

And at one point it very nearly was. My platoon was out on the Beacons. Two days and nights out in the wild mountains without support, and around twenty-five tortuous miles to cover with infantry manoeuvres thrown in. Some pace. Day two found us wet and cold, doing our darndest to meet the deadline, when Private Casson folded. He'd been game enough at the start, but the cold had got to him. He was soaking wet, and hypothermia—exposure—had set in. In these things the most crucial thing is to stay dry, even in the worst wet—rain, rivers, sodden campsites, you must keep your inner clothing dry if humanly possible. He hadn't managed it, and the cold had got to him. His internal body temperature had started to fall towards the fatal limit, and he was fading fast.

Staggering around and making no sense whatever. (Exhausted men can still talk sense.) Casson was rambling. The 'P Company' sergeant who met us at the checkpoint was all sympathy.

'Keep him going, sir. He'll make it. Just keep him going. You've got to make the summit by 20 00 hours or you'll all dip out.'

I had done a pilot's survival course, and remembered the signs. I knew that if his temperature had dropped beyond the limit then no amount of exercise could raise it. But I was in poor shape myself. Was I making sense?

'Sergeant, Casson's got hypothermia.'

'Just keep him going. He'll get there. You'll see, sir. Just keep him going.'

My own head was spinning with lack of sleep, aching limbs, and a conflict of interest. Either to try to keep him going by will-power, if that were possible, and get to the rendezvous, or attend to him here and now. One thought kept drumming through my head: 'An officer's duty is to his men.' The Hampshires had taught me that as an infantry officer. I, not the sergeant, was responsible for this man, 'P Company' or no 'P Company'. I made my decision.

'Stuff this for a game of soldiers. This one's had it Sergeant, and if you can't see that then you'd better get off the mountain!'

'Careful, sir. We don't want to lose points, do we?'

I ignored him, and in the lee of a dry-stone wall called a halt.

'Stove!' I ordered. A hexamine field stove was produced.

'Matches!' I set about trying to light it for a warming drink. Soup, tea, anything.

'Get out the sleeping-bag. Get him dry, and get him in it.' The rest of the squad did as ordered. One stripped off Casson's socks and boots, and warmed Casson's bare and battered feet under his arms. Another snuggled the thermal sleeping-bag around him. It was our last resort against the cold.

'In with him,' I continued. Another soldier slid in, and gripped his mate in an embrace holding him close to himself, transmitting the warmth of his body.

I struck on with the matches. But they wouldn't take. They were all blowing out in the strong wind no matter how I shielded them, burning my fingers in the process. I was cold and shaking too, and the sudden bite of the flame made me drop the whole lot more than once. The sergeant sneered, unconvinced.

'This is all taking time, sir.' Pressure again. He'd been doing this job too long.

'Lord,' I said under my breath, 'please. The matches, or I think this man will die.'

The very last match flashed into flame, and the hexamine fuel cube caught, and burnt up brightly on its thin metal base, growling bluely as the gusty wind tore at the tiny conflagration. But it stayed alight. Very soon a hot drink was being offered up to the white senseless lips of the dangerously chilled soldier. Slowly his spirit returned. He began to moan. A sign of conscious awareness. A good sign. I gave him twenty minutes. By now even the sergeant was quiet. Then I hauled Casson to his feet.

'We're moving on. Drake, take his pack.'

'Sir.'

We staggered on uphill. The nightmare still had ten days to run. Casson dropped out before the end. But at least he was alive to tell the tale.

Mary and I learned a lot about each other on 'P Company'. She would receive me through the door on the nights I did get home as a pile of exhausted flesh and bones loosely knit together by filthy combat gear, and topped by a stunned and little-boy-lost smile. A walking wreck whose only future was the six o'clock alarm for another day of punishment. Strong-smelling liniment was the universal balm for the battered, bruised and bleeding feet after another day running and jumping. She applied it faithfully, with calmness and conviction.

'Only another two weeks,' she would say. 'You're doing fine. The platoon's doing fine. You're still very fit. You can go on!'

And I did. At least she meant it. Unlike the sergeants. Even today Mary cannot smell that embrocation without instantly recollecting piles of smelly socks, combat gear and sweat. She did 'P Company' too. She kept me steady and level. And this was, all said and done, only an exercise. But she and I learned about ourselves. And that learning was crucial for the future. Jesus may not have been sending me down the weather forecast, but he was at work all the while.

And for Alan and I, getting through had become very personal. At stake was not a job in the army, or even a place among the elite paras. We both had that already—unlike many who depended on their 'P Company' success to start or build their careers. No, to us, it was simply to show we were not the inferiors we had been made out to be over a year of ribbing and jibes. 'Penguin, ha.' Muttered behind our backs with a jerk of the thumb. For us it *was* mind over matter. It mattered. We grew to respect and like each other a great deal. And Alan was always one to quiz my Christian heart too.

'And just how's Jesus going to pull you out of this one?' he'd throw at me when I'd bought the short straw to lead over the assault course, or whatever. I'd reply evenly that I thought he probably would, one way or the other. And often we'd talk late into the night about these things as a result of his pointed remarks. But that was mainly later, back on the Squadron. On 'P Company' at night, we slept.

They were sneaky, too, on 'P Company'. In testing us. Sometimes things were lined up to see if you had flexibility, and could take charge when things which weren't planned cropped up. Especially when you were tired.

On one ten-mile run, we had completed most of it, and were approaching one of the last of the inevitable series of windswept mountain ridges to have our names ticked off to prove we'd passed through, when the clipboard manager—who was actually the commanding officer's driver—casually commented that he didn't know how but he'd managed to get the CO's Landrover stuck in a ditch.

The platoon commander before us laughed, and said that that was his bad luck. A recovery vehicle was no doubt on its way. And he doubled his men off on the next timed leg. Some of us though, seeing we would have to live with the CO for the coming weeks, rallied the tired troops around, and heave-ho—out it came in one lift. No sign of the CO. But a suitably thankful driver.

Back at base camp that night one or two platoon commanders began sharing the trials of the day.

'Do y'know, on that last ridge, CO's driver'd put the 'rover in a ditch. Idiot. Thought he'd have known better...'

'Funny. We found the CO's 'rover in a ditch too...'

'So did we...'

We began to realize we'd been had. It was a set-up. Next day when the points were announced, platoon commanders who had sorted the vehicle out got a bonus. Those who had suggested the driver 'waited for a man who could' did not. Paras are supposed to fix their own problems.

The worst for me, though, was not the rugged hills. It was the assault course. What did it for me was the height. I just couldn't take it. Bashing through water and swinging from ropes was OK. But height. Oh, no. I began to know fear. The worst was the aptly named 'confidence' course eighty feet up in the trees. It needed more than a song from Julie Andrews to get me over this one. A continuous sequence of walkways and swings, planks and jumps.

And the end was a spring into space with the aim of landing, clawing desperately, on a net suspended vertically.

The second time around I stopped dead. At the edge of the jump. I just couldn't do it. The sergeants were screaming. The platoon was pushing up behind. But I simply couldn't make it. You had to look out and down to judge it. The moment I'd looked down, I'd frozen.

I thought I had blown it. Dipped 'P Company'. But at the review my points were up on other parts, so they let me go on. But they knew there was a weakness there. So did I. And if it was left unconquered—then I would never make a para. Time would tell.

A memory of one morning comes back to me specially from that time. Mary and I were sitting down before dawn at our breakfast table—I, still very tired despite a night's sleep, muscles aching, feet throbbing, wolfing food down to give me energy for the day. I was taking a moment for thought and prayer before meeting the crashing impact of another 'P Company' day. My Bible was lying open among the coffee cups. A verse came to mind. I riffled through to the words of the Old Testament prophet Isaiah—a man who understood taking the tough option:

'They that wait upon God shall renew their strength. They shall mount up with wings like eagles . . .'

Yes. That was what I really needed to make it as a para. New strength. And, come to that, wings might come in handy too.

'Make it so for me, Lord,' I murmured, deadly serious. And he did. I passed out of 'P Company' with Alan.

But I still had to jump to get my wings, my paratroop wings. I could wear the coveted red beret, but not the wings. And the wings I had to have. I started losing sleep. What the sergeants hadn't managed, the jumping did. Mental pressure. I was right on the edge. The static balloon. That was the killer. The dreadful feeling of falling, helpless, for two hundred feet before anything happened. Just stepping into thin air.

Terror stalked those weeks. I tossed and moaned in bed. Lay awake sleepless. Mary and I have always prayed together as a couple, but earnest were the prayers on the mornings of a jump.

I hated all of those qualifying jumps. The first jump, the second... two from the balloon, and then six more from an aircraft. Jumping from the aircraft was never quite so bad as from the static balloon. For a start, you were shut up inside until it came to going, and then you were shuffled through the door so fast you didn't have time to think. Plummeting downwards was avoided. You plummeted backwards instead—in the buffeting 110-knot slip-stream of the jump aircraft. Made it a bit easier. The others used to laugh at me in the back of the lumbering RAF Hercules transports as we flew around waiting for the drop. The only pilot in the jump, and as sick as a dog. I always was. Right in the bag.

The main danger from aircraft jumps is tangled rigging lines. The slip-stream can catch you, and spin you around. Too much of a twist as you leave, and your chute won't open properly. Then you have to stabilize yourself before pulling your reserve. Peace-time exercise jumps are around eight hundred feet, and you always carry a reserve 'chute. That gives you just over a second-and-a-half to decide if you need it. Not long. The other danger—in mass drops—is taking someone else's air. Looking up, if you see boots scrabbling across your canopy you know someone is in trouble. With height they might make it back into clear air. Near the ground, losing air and dropping fast means breaking a leg, or worse.

Much later I was often tasked, with my helicopter, as Drop Zone medical cover to fly injured paras back to hospital. I was always needed. Someone always hurt something. Not many, fortunately, through failed 'chutes. It was usually bad or awkward landings. Ankle sprains, broken bones occasionally. I only ever saw one 'whistle in' as we called it. He had left the aircraft spinning, and had got so tangled that he'd twisted his emergency 'chute as well.

The worst jump I ever attended was Kiel. It was a major peace-time disaster. A full divisional drop, at night, with hundreds of men in the air, plus vehicles, support troops—the works. The jump height was increased by two hundred feet to give an extra safety margin. In the event it cost some men their lives. The height increase was decided without proper notification to the DZs, and the jump target drift was calculated using the old height. The first jumpers from each aircraft therefore drifted well past the Drop Zone before landing. They landed in the commercial ship channel. The Kiel Canal. Paratroopers expecting to land on firm ground suddenly found themselves battling for their lives in freezing water in the dark among the merciless steel hulls of passing shipping. Eighteen men died. Some became entangled under their 'chutes, and drowned. Some were pulled into propellers. Some just could not swim. It was so bad that in the end I just landed my machine on the bank, and joined the rescuers, army and civilian, in the mud—desperately pulling exhausted men from the water.

I did the jumps. I don't know how. But I was sure as pleased as punch just to be wearing the parachute wings and the red beret at last. And, as an unexpected bonus, I was told I was to convert on to the army's other light helicopter. An all-British machine called the Scout. Turbine jet-engined. Fast, manoeuvrable, and capable of carrying passengers, it was a treat to fly. On the conversion course Dave Rowat went through some time ahead of me, and so became my Scout mentor following the brief re-training period.

As we met on the tarmac, he stood stiffly to attention. I was a little taken aback.

'Morning, Sergeant,' I grinned.

'Good morning, sah!' The hand shot up to the forehead with unaccustomed precision. In the air arm of the army, formalities between pilots are usually relatively relaxed.

I returned the salute as best I could. He eased up, and took my hand.

'*Very* good to serve with you again, sir. Well done.'

I realized I was the baby subaltern no more. Now I was his accepted officer. Now I wore paratroop wings. A warm glow crept through me. After that our informality increased. And so did the respect. On both sides.

8

Second Tour

I swung the Scout in over the perimeter wire at Aldergrove, and landed, hover-taxiing across to the dispersal
on the military side of the airfield. It was familiar
territory. Yet much had changed. The situation in 1974
was more tense. The terrorists had become more sophisticated, and so had we. The different, more capable,
helicopter I was now flying would widen the scope of the
job considerably. With better intelligence and better
equipment we all hoped we would soon see the end of
the troubles, with the army dealing with the extremists,
thus leaving the way open for an equitable political
solution.

Yes. We really believed it possible. I believed the army
had an important anti-terrorist job to do in the province.
And that we would do it, wrap it up and win. It may be
difficult to understand from the outside, but we were
putting our lives on the line daily. We had to believe it was
worth it. That we would gain something for the sacrifice.

I fluttered in towards the upraised bats of the mar-
shaller by the hangar. He was a squadron para. As I
manoeuvred into the flight line in response to his signals, I couldn't fail to notice the remarkable sun-glasses he
was wearing. They were day-glo pink, with fitted eye-
brows. I felt perhaps they were not service issue. The
soldier drew his bat across his throat to indicate I was
down in position, and could cut my engine. Then he

approached and stuck his head into the cockpit.

'Wotch-er, sir! Hear you're a real para now, sir!'

'Morning, Private Crawley. And what do you call those?'

'Ah, that's just to keep the currant bun out of me mince pies, sir!'

It was good to be back on the squadron.

Working with a much more powerful turbine machine gave me a whole new perspective on life. I could range further and go faster—and also I could carry troops. The routines now were Border Patrol and Eagle Patrol. The former was just what it said—following every twist and turn of the invisible line which marked out British territory from that of Eire. Looking for transgressors. Staying in UK was an almost impossible task. I crossed the line endlessly, unintentionally and often unnoticeably. Anyone in a position to spot my errors was probably just as confused as I as to where the real border lay.

I remember one occasion when I dropped a 'stick' (section) of 'toms' (infantrymen) off for a border foot-patrol—the Scout could carry four at a time, five if I didn't take an air gunner. It was Indian country. There was low cloud so I decided to go off for a wander rather than stay around low and noisy in hostile country as a target. They would soon let me know on the net if they wanted out. One of the little jobs that I was supposed to do when at a loose end was fertilizer inspection—flying low over farms and checking the brand names on the sacks. Certain fertilizers, with a high nitrogen content, were banned, and farmers could be arrested for having them. So off I spun in the murk, nipping up around the farms, scaring the chickens and checking sacks in the farmyards.

Twenty minutes later up came the stick leader saying could they move on. Round I went and pulled up over the ridge where I had left them and . . . there was no one there. I hovered for a minute, completely baffled. No, they said, they hadn't moved. Where was I?

I took a hasty look at the map, and moved on across the ridge. Mm, town with twin spires. There. Possibly that one on the map. I moved on a mile. Small village. No, that shouldn't be there. Not familiar at all. My eye wandered down the map. Across the border. Now *there* was a town and village. *Five miles* into the South! Brain engaged with a rush and, pushing the cyclic into the instrument panel and pulling the collective into my armpit, I sped north, turbine screaming. Soon I had my hill in sight, and four men on board.

'What kept you, sir?' asked the patrol NCO.

'Oh, watching the navigation. Can't rush. There's a lot of Ireland out there.'

'How do you know where the border is from up here, sir?'

'Experience, really. That's all. Just experience.'

A warning came out soon after that. Any trespassing over the line meant instant recall to the UK. I nearly thought of having another go.

But Eagle Patrol was best. Up would come ops: 'Suspect proceeding in white Cortina, Mike Kilo November Fife Fife Four, heading south on A24 to Newry. Eagle intercept. Over.'

'Roger. Eagle is Army Five Seven. On my way. Out.'

For some reason, it was always a white Cortina. If they'd banned the lot of them I'm sure the hoods couldn't have driven anything else.

I would spin down from my patrol height and, with the Ordnance Survey road map on my knee, pin-point the road, and choose a decent place to intercept the car. The idea was to fly past and overtake the suspect vehicle unseen, choose a place to land ahead of him, plump down in the road, and be there ready and waiting, an instant check-point with guns levelled, when he came screeching around the corner. Great.

This worked fine a lot of the time, but often the roads

were country lanes, and too narrow to land the Scout in. Then you had to find an adjacent field, and get the lads out in time for them to be impressively strung across the road when the car came around. This was more difficult. Finding a suitable field, with access to road, *and* in time. There was also another hazard which threatened us all at one time or another. I had zipped ahead and chosen a field. The timing was tight, and the white roof of the suspect was less than a mile away. I came around from behind a line of trees, bursting into view with the intention of slamming the machine down the last thirty feet to the deck. With only twenty feet to go, my air gunner shouted: 'Wires, wires, *wires*!'

I looked up from my aiming-point to see two sets of almost invisible telephone cables stretching right across the field. The suspect car snarled gleefully around the corner as I pulled up harder on the collective than Private Crawley doing a handbrake turn in the CO's Landrover. The machine bucked as though kicked from behind. We skimmed over the wires with the transmission over-torque warning horn screaming in my ears. I eased back on to the ground. The white Cortina was a puff of blue exhaust in the downland countryside.

The stick leader put his head around the cockpit door. 'Can't we follow 'em, sir?

'Strained the engine with that last manoeuvre, soldier,' I replied. 'Got to have it looked at before I go anywhere else. Best secure the area.'

He got the toms out, disappointed. I called ops, and we snuggled down defensively in the field, heads down and weapons up, chewing Irish daisies until another Scout arrived with the Squadron REME technicians on board. 'Tut, tut, tut,' was written all over their faces as they prodded and poked and deliberated. They looked like builders about to quote for repairing a rotten ceiling. In the end they said it was safe to fly back empty. Later, after tests, they scrapped the whole gear-box. One up to the hoods. An expensive gearbox wrecked, and not even a Cortina to show for it.

I often thought about it that way, remembering what the major had said at my first briefing. Almost by definition the terrorist has the upper hand. In order to score, he has only to make you fail a little in your duty.

On one occasion I remember a young lad with a little airgun who put another machine out of action. I was transporting a group of senior officers to an operations conference, and we had just taken off when one of them spotted someone in a field brandishing what looked like a machine pistol.

'Down,' ordered the colonel. Down I went. Out jumped the colonel, a half-colonel, and two majors, pistols drawn, teeth bared, tally-ho-ing for all they were worth.

'Let's get him!' was the last thing I heard the Colonel utter as they left the aircraft faster than a stick of toms. Then I was left with a problem. I was sitting on the deck in bandit country, possibly the principal target of a 'come on', being the only transport for my illustrious hunting party. I didn't intend waiting around. I reached for the collective, and was about to get airborne when I noticed that no one had bothered to close the rear doors. Lack of breeding, I call it. I couldn't lift off with unsecured doors. I reached over, and quickly pulled the emergency release. Two lovely new doors fell off and smashed themselves to pieces on the grass. I lifted. Safe at two thousand feet I was concerned to notice the turbine outlet temperature indicator moving towards the red. Funny. Still, I could pull power, and it seemed to stabilize after a while.

Down below, I could see the brass-hats' impromptu sally had been successful, and a young lad with what turned out to be an airgun had been apprehended and was being handed over to a rather astonished and over-awed foot patrol of Light Infantry who had now deployed comfortingly around the landing site. I dropped back in.

Shutting down to wait for the A-Team to finish congratulating themselves on a good show, I wandered around to the back of the Scout. The high turbine temperature reading was on my mind. And there, sticking out of the engine intake housing, was the remains of an Ordnance Survey army map, plastic covered, staff-officers-for-the-use-of. One of my esteemed passengers in his enthusiasm for action had popped his map case down conveniently on a nearby ledge—just behind my engine intake. A later report showed that twenty-seven compressor blades had been damaged. One machine grounded and two doors smashed. All with an airgun. Sharp work.

But it wasn't always my seniors whom I had problems with. If the Paras couldn't find trouble, they made it up for themselves. One evening I had a call from the RAF police at the gate reporting that a patrol had picked up Privates Crawley and Eden outside the Para-Dice Club on the base. The name indicates the style. They were taking them into the cooler just to, ah, cool off. They had both had one too many, and the patrol had wanted to avoid trouble.

As they were my responsibility, I hopped into the Landrover, and sped down to the provost marshal's office to discover it strangely quiet. I knocked on the— necessarily stout—door. No smartly gaitered and belted airforce lawman appeared. I rang the bell. Still there was nothing. There were certainly lights on inside, and I could hear the sounds of movement and voices. But nothing happened. I bent to the door.

'Er, Lieutenant Marflect, 664 Para Squadron,' I called out respectfully. The base police could make life hard for you if you got on their wrong side. Extra ID card checks, vehicle checks, all that kind of thing. Suddenly the door sprang open, and the massive bulk of Private Eden filled the entrance.

'Why didn't you say, sir? All that ringing. We thought it was more scuffers.'

I noticed that Private Eden had a sub-machine-gun slung around his neck.

I entered, and he stood courteously, if unsteadily, aside. Inside the brightly-lit strong room stood six RAF policemen. They stood up against the wall. In a line. They had their hands on their heads. The other side of the desk sat Private Crawley, another sub-machine-gun resting in his arms, the barrel waving gently in the direction of the half-dozen guardians of military law.

'Shall I shoot 'em now, sir, or lock 'em up till later?' came the cockney enquiry as he lurched to his feet.

Choking back laughter, I ordered him and Eden to put up their guns, and quick march into the cells. The relieved policemen recovered their weapons. It had not been their evening.

'Aw, sir. It was just a joke. Don't be too hard on 'em,' grinned Crawley as the cell door clanged shut, leaving them to dry out for the night.

I asked the rueful RAF what had happened. One of their patrol had had trouble climbing back up into his truck after collecting the 'prisoners' outside the Club; these 'prisoners' had kindly offered to give him a hand up. They'd take his gun first, if that would help. Next thing he knew, there was a steel barrel in the neck with a mean soldier on the end of it. The RAF were extremely grateful for my appearance. I have to say that after that small incident I had very little trouble with the police on the base.

Sometimes, though, things were rather more grim. Like the time I put a stick of troops down right on top of a car bomb. The whole set up was a 'come on'. Ops thought it might be, but anything that is amiss has to be checked out. You just try to take precautions. I had dropped the small section down in a field by an abandoned car. The registration indicated it was stolen so it had to be checked. I cautioned the stick leader.

'Corporal, don't approach it. Just search the area around. Head down, weapons up, right?'

'Sir.'

Down I went, and out they piled. I pulled pitch, and lifted up over the trees. The blast rocked me where I flew, slewing the machine across the sky. I hit the radio button, screaming for help. Controlling the machine in the tortured air, I fought for height, and checked the controls and instruments. Nothing seemed damaged. Ops alerted, I jabbed the frequency selector to call ground. I feared the worst.

The corporal came back shaken, but clear.

'The car blew, sir ... just exploded in front of us. I don't ...'

'Casualties?'

'All OK, I think. No, wait. Roberts is going into shock I think, sir. Can we can get him out?'

I could not believe no one had been injured. The blast had been a powerful one. But shock can be serious if not treated, so I brought the machine in low at the edge of the field. The smoke from the bomb swished away in my rotorwash, revealing the car blasted into a million pieces lying all around a now fiercely burning chassis. The corporal and another soldier appeared carrying the Fusilier. He was shaking, incredibly white under his dark skin—he was a black soldier—and rigid, in deep shock. But fortunately not incapable of sitting.

Med-evac patients who are prostrate normally have to travel outside the helicopter in a coffin-shaped container on the skids. In fact it is so coffin-like we had to put a notice inside saying 'You Are Not In A Coffin' in case some poor evacuee regained consciousness inside, and thought he had been prematurely buried!

As the man was being strapped in I turned around and prized his rifle out of his tight grasp. I checked it for ammunition while they strapped him in. Full magazine and one up the spout. A dangerous state for a gun indeed. I ejected the round, and glanced along the barrel. It was out of true. The force of the blast had actually bent the barrel. Fortunately, the man had not tried to shoot with it, or shock would have been the least of his problems. I took off for hospital. At least the corporal had done what was ordered. Heads down and weapons up.

When we looked over the site later we found that the car had been packed with explosives, and set off by a man hiding in the bushes. He had calmly waited for me to land, drop the Fusiliers and take off again, blowing the charge when he thought the squad close enough to catch the blast. I had actually landed across the wires, buried in the grass, which triggered it. A cool customer.

Putting troops down cold—with no one on the ground already—was always a risky business. We did it occasionally with a small force on the Eagle patrols. If ops called for larger numbers, then the RAF had to do it. They had the larger Puma machine which could carry up to nineteen troops in one go. A much better force to deliver. But there were restrictions. They wouldn't operate at night without a prepared landing zone. That meant either men on the ground already, or guess-who going in ahead.

It worked like this: we would get airborne with a designer n-million-candle-power searchlight affair strapped underneath the helicopter. It was called Night Sun, and, as the name implies, gave instant daylight. It was so powerful we had to have extra generators put on the helicopter to run it. Then we would meet up with the RAF Pumas which would formate on us to get to the target. They would tuck in close. Really close. How close? If I tell you that the way they formated was by using the dimmed lights on *my* instrument panel, then you've some idea. Normally, to help a bit, I'd pull the fuse on my fuel-boost warning light, and the red winking of that would be enough for them to fly on. It was a tight formation. Then I'd set up my Decca Radio Navigator, and we'd fly off on 'Dectrack' into the darkness. When my Decca gave the right coordinates I'd get my gunner to hit the switch and, hey presto! the appropriate field would be bathed in limelight, and in would go the RAF. It played the devil with your night vision, but at least they could see where to land.

One way and another we helped the RAF out quite a lot that way. One para observer thought we did it rather too much, and quietly fitted a cut-out crab over the lens of his pilot's Night Sun. When they next turned it on a giant crab was projected on to the ground in the middle of the landing field. It looked like Batman had arrived. The RAF were not amused. Protests went up, and the sticker came off. No sense of humour those crabs. The inter-service name for the RAF is 'crabs' by the way. I've no idea why. We, the army, are 'the army', and the navy are 'fish-heads'. OK, if you must know, the army are called 'pongos'. Don't mention it.

Night Sun was a very useful item, but it had one drawback. If you were using it at any height, perhaps doing an area search for an arms dump or a hidden vehicle, and you flew into cloud, then the back glare was so bright that if your air gunner didn't kill the light instantly, you had a white-out in the cockpit. Loss of control and a terminal dive was usually the unfortunate and sharp conclusion.

The knock at my door was insistent. I groped out of the mists of sleep, and looked at my watch. It was eight o'clock. It was my roster off, and Sunday morning. What was the mess room steward about?

'Yes?' I yelled impatiently.

'Sir, the OC wants you down at ops right away. Someone's gone down.'

Quickly I pulled on my working uniform—in live operations the all-in-one flying suits were replaced by para smocks and boots. I ran down from the mess. As I crashed through the ops room door, I heard the duty signaller's chilling words: 'Can you confirm the pilot is dead? Over.'

'Confirmed.'

'Roger. Out.'

The OC was by him. He turned grimly to me. It's Rowat, I'm afraid, David. Went down near Portadown. Rifle fire, we think. He was very low.'

'But we have to be low!' I blurted, stunned. Dave Rowat dead? My cheerful paratroop guide for over four years. The sergeant whose jibes had put me up to 'P Company', and who had treated me as 'the boss' when I'd made it through. Who'd taught me almost all the smart flying I knew. Rowat dead?

We had recently been told of a threat from shoulder-launched ground-to-air missiles. So we had been ordered to work below the tree-line wherever we could. That meant we were more liable to take hits from small arms. Dave had been required to be low.

'David!' The OC broke in firmly, controlling his own emotions as well as mastering mine. 'Get up there. Now. Take over from him.' He paused. 'See what you can do,' he ended.

I turned and made for my machine, pulling on my flak jacket in the corner of the hangar while the ground crew pre-flighted the aircraft. I tapped my holster, and picked up my sub-machine-gun. Those hoods had better not be anywhere near when I came by. Just a glimmer, that's all I needed, and I would be all over them. They wouldn't know what hit them. I put a couple of extra magazines on the seat beside me, and pulled on my green helmet and flying gloves. My hands were sweating as I fired up the turbine.

I hugged—and I mean hugged—the contours all the way out to Portadown, torque on the stops. Power-wound all the way up, saying nothing. When I got there they stopped me from landing. Overfly, they said. The area wasn't safe. They were right. From me, it wasn't. Woe betide anyone who put their nose out of a bush even an inch. They would know it wasn't safe.

I was told to clear the area, and wait on the ground at Gough Barracks in Armagh. I landed and stood by. Eventually I got the call to go back. The area was secure. How they could say that when anyone could shoot up at me from a clump of trees, a bush or a building, I don't know. But they were doing their best, I knew. They weren't the enemy. Just doing their best, in an unreal situation.

I arrived overhead, and hovered purposefully, fish-tailing the machine from side to side and bouncing up and down. Ducking and weaving in the air. Hoping to provoke a reaction. Looking out for flashes. Looking in bushes. Looking in windows. Trying not to look at the twisted remains of a helicopter just like my own right below me.

A cordon had been drawn around, and in the surrounding field I could see a platoon of Fusiliers had taken up defensive positions. I plunged into the centre of the ring next to David's mashed machine. The gaping smashed door of his cockpit rattled and banged in my downwash. Through the broken glass of the canopy I could see a figure still inside, helmet resting awkwardly on the panel. No living man could sit like that. He sat where he had crashed across the controls.

I landed and shut down. The platoon commander ran up. 'Dead,' he confirmed. Dave had been left there deliberately. Any accident must be left undisturbed until all relevant evidence has been collected. The accident inspectors had just left.

'Help me with him,' I replied. And together we eased Dave clear of the scrunching metal and glass wreckage that had been his cockpit. Outside I gently slid his helmet off. The pugnacious, ready smile seemed to look up out of the crumpled features. But it was my imagination. He was dead cold. I manhandled him over to my machine, and laid him on the stretcher base, pulling the blanket over. I told ops what I was about, and took off for Belfast.

I landed in the hospital grounds, and was bundled into an ambulance alongside him for a trip through the city to the morgue. I had to personally identify the body. Cleaned up and laid out in his chunky para clothing he looked more the sort of man I had known. I touched the white parachute and blue wings on his smock—the symbol that had brought us together. As a para he was now strangely defenceless. I set my features, murmured something irrelevant, and was driven back to my helicopter by the same ambulance.

I started up, and flew back to Aldergrove, emotionally exhausted. I staggered across to the mess, and up into the room I had left so hurriedly that morning, pitched over on to the bed, and lay there. Then, uncontrollably and profoundly, I began to cry until my whole body was convulsed with great racking sobs. Shocked and bereaved and horrified, I gave way to the anger and sadness of the day. Then, mercifully, amid the tears came sleep. Even for a para, it seemed, there was still pain.

9
Trade

Swiftly and expertly Moondi ran the sharp knife across
the pig's throat. In a convulsion of death the animal
coughed blood, and sank to the ground. It was a neat
job. Moondi stood up and called to his wife Dukwe.
Obediently she came out of his hut and, taking the rear
legs, pulled out the pig so that he could set about
butchering it along its length. Though strictly speaking
it was food preparation, something normally done by
women, pig butchery was always performed by the man.

Killing the pig was traditionally associated with feast-
ing and tribal formalities. Not only that, the head of the
household whose pig it was would then be able to make a
choice of the best cuts for himself. Those rippling with
succulent, mobile fat. But though Moondi cut the pig
today with care, he took trouble over it for a different
reason. In fact he was not quite sure how he should
prepare it. For the first time in his life the pig which lay
under his knife that morning would not be part of his meal
that night. It was a strange feeling. Cutting up a pig you
were not going to eat.

Moondi was used to butchering to taste. He knew
intimately who in his family would expect what from
the carcase. He himself would get the fatty thighs and
neck. He had a special liking for the neck. To his father he
gave part of the back, for his two elderly uncles he
reserved forelegs, and his dozens of cousins always took

slices, admittedly rather meaty slices—there was still some fat to be had—from the belly.

Butchering for the family was easy. Doing it for strangers was unexpectedly hard. His pig was going for trade. For the first time in Hupla experience the pig would be taken out of the valley to be cooked and eaten by someone else. Someone he didn't know, nor was ever likely to. The newly appointed Tribal Representative of the Distant Chief (who, they discovered, claimed some sort of jurisdiction over the valley) had requested this. Since the representative was in fact Moondi's brother, Kwalogo, he had appointed Moondi to be the first supplier. It was supposed to be a brotherly favour—and he was not, in truth, unhappy to accept it.

Moondi knew it was something that happened regularly in other valleys. More importantly, he also knew that in return he would get trading discs. Discs which could be exchanged for Durables: highly desirable crafted artefacts brought into the newly cleared landing ground by the flying winged carriers. All the same, it felt very strange. A great many things were strange nowadays, he concluded, as he deftly hacked away at the distended carcase with his knife. Indeed the knife itself, though he was now used to it, was one of the strangest. A Durable made of a shiny material, bright like running water, but as hard as stone, and yet able to be sharpened like wood, it could cut along its whole length (except where it was secured into a handle) with the sharpness of a new arrow point, and it would go on and on doing so for cut after cut.

The knife had transformed so many of the daily chores of life. How had they managed for so long with sharp sticks and edged cutting stones? From harvesting sweet potatoes to cutting grass-thatch for the huts the bright-stone knife was fast and accurate, and now indispensable. This was just the sort of Durable that Moondi could exchange discs for. He particularly had his eye on a bright-stone hatchet. He wondered just how many discs that would require.

Durable hatchets, trading discs, carriers, remote over-lords ... it was amazing what things had happened. Of course the winged carriers were the key. He had learned that.

As he worked away at the pig, Moondi thought back to that violent and tragic day when the tribe had heard the carrier's intrusive noise for the first time. It had been louder than any cacophony of drums at a feast. It had been the day of the battle, the day that Lanya had died. Lanya. He looked down at the quiescent female figure at his feet quietly packaging the meat. Dukwe was not Lanya, nor were Mu-lew or Folukwe. They were all his wives. True they were pretty. His status as High Elder's son, and his associated wealth had ensured he could afford the best. But they were not like Lanya. He did not know why.

These other wives performed as well as she. In every way. But they were just wives. Workers of his household, bearers of his children, adornment of his status, and indicators of his wealth. They had cost good pigs. But what Lanya had had, and had meant, was something that he had come to suspect could not be bought with pigs. He didn't know what it was, except that it hurt to be reminded of it. There was a pang now, an unnamed, soulful longing.

On that dreadful day, he had known—somehow, his spirit's sensitivity unbearably heightened by the shocks of the day—that the roaring over-flight of the carrier was linked to the tribal destiny. But he knew not why. Now, much later, with new wives and growing children, he was beginning to see something of this outworking.

For many days afterward, the people had talked of the bird-like shape which had rushed down upon them, flying the length of the valley, darting and swooping as if about to consume the celebrating, victorious villagers. Some had suggested that this was the flying spirit of the offended ancestor fearfully departing. A consequence of Moondi's bloody victory. Others, especially the Spirit

Talkers, had proclaimed it a new god-spirit to whom service should be offered, and had drawn up plans to prepare a wood-and-thatch replica, based on the best and clearest reports they could gather within the village. This they intended to peg out in a clearing beside the huts in case it returned. Then, at least, it would know it was recognized and respected.

But these plans had been forestalled by the arrival in the village, shortly after, of the first Pale People.

Moondi had been leading a small hunting party, looking for wildfowl to season a meal or two. They had moved some way out of the valley into Dani country. They hadn't really meant to travel that far, but game had been scarce on the hunt, and he didn't think the Dani generally came to this extremity of their territory. The Dani would probably never know. And, even if they did, he and his hunters would be in and out before they could do anything about it.

So they were surprised when they heard the distinctive noises of a party of warriors making their way towards them along the jungle trail. On a swift signal from Moondi the Hupla had melted smoothly into the jungle to wait. Either they would launch an ambush, though that would not be wise on Dani territory, or they would quietly watch them pass on by, and then steal away, avoiding the trail, back to their own hunting forest. Moondi knew that any bloodshed would almost certainly lead to reprisal raids, and a lengthy tribal vendetta. He was not authorized to start such a conflict, even had there been warrant, so he resolved to wait with his party quietly under cover.

Suddenly a man began to call loudly through the jungle in the Hupla tongue. 'Ho! Ho-ah! Brave Hupla hunting warriors, fierce ones of the High Valleys, I am Gatti of the Dani people. Answer me! Ho, ho-ah! We are not here to call battle nor advance a raid. We bear only hunting weapons! Answer me!'

Moondi was astounded. How did the Dani know that the Hupla hunted on their territory, and were there at that moment? His plans of escape were wrecked. Intrigued by the formal but unusual summons, he stepped quickly out of the undergrowth and on to the path, bow strung and ready. His hunting party followed.

It was the Dani's turn to be surprised. They had known Hupla to be hunting in the area, for they had watched the movement of the game birds above the trees from the thin lofty watch-towers, built uniquely by the Dani, which commanded far-reaching views over the jungle beyond their villages. But they had not expected to find them quite so close.

There was a tense pause as the opposing parties eyed each other nervously. Both wrong-footed. Then Moondi had noticed the Pale People. Two of the strangest people he had ever seen were standing with the Dani party. His first thought was that they were ghosts or war-spirits fighting for the Dani, and he dropped into a crouch, the defensive firing position for close quarters. Gatti, seeing their reaction and guessing the cause, shouted, 'Stand! Hold your fire! They are men like us. They breathe. Their skin is pale—that is all!'

Moondi stood up. 'Why have you called for the Hupla? And why do you hunt in company with pale strangers?' he snapped imperiously.

The bilingual Dani replied calmly but brightly, apparently unangered by Moondi's aggressive posture and sharp question. 'We have some news, brought by these, the pale people, but also by ourselves, concerning the nature of things outside the High Valleys. We have particular news of the winged carriers, which come like large birds that drum and roar. The Hupla warriors have, no doubt, seen and heard these?'

Moondi was nonplussed. It was the strangest communication he had ever heard. The Dani were obviously on an errand of some significance, and the two ghostly

strangers added weight to his surprising statement. He
had to admit that ghostly people were most likely to be
bound up in the bird-spirit that had roared over the huts
that fateful day. He also respected the Dani. They were
men of the High Valleys, too.

In the end, after more discussion, Moondi consented to
return to his village, escorting the curious expedition. The
Elders of the tribe—including his father—and the Spirit
Talkers were the experts on such matters. They could
decide what to do. If by chance any treachery was
contemplated they could easily overpower the little Dani
force, pale people notwithstanding.

On the journey Moondi studied the pale people closely
(as did all his comrades), fascinated and revolted at the
same time. Then they had all, in turn, hesitantly moved up
to touch and feel them—their light skin and shiny fair
hair—to try the strength of the Dani's claim that they were
actual living beings, not shades of the dead. They had not
seemed to mind. Their faces were extraordinarily pale,
but not, as the Hupla had first thought, in death. There
was real life in the wan skin. It just wasn't like theirs. The
strangeness of the pale people was doubly enhanced by
their mysterious insistence on encumbering themselves
with what Moondi took at the time to be animal skins but
which, he had learned later, were soft woven vegetable
fibres. These woven fibres were as soft as chicken down,
and hung all over the pale people, except for their bare
arms. Worse, the Hupla discovered the pale people wore
no gourd.

Moondi smiled to himself at the memory of it, continuing to slice up the slippery meat into what he guessed
would be edible family portions, tossing them to Dukwe
who carefully wrapped them up in soft green banana
leaves before adding them to the growing pile of packaged meat at her feet. He glanced down at his own wide
and stumpy, practical everyday gourd. Perhaps he would
go in and change it before the winged carrier arrived. The

first pig to be carried out of the valley deserved some ceremony.

Finding that the strangers wore no gourds had been truly offensive. It was an insult to make a formal visit, or conduct a special expedition—which this evidently was—without sporting a distinctive, impressive gourd. And the strangers' drapery had concealed this disturbing fact until quite some time down the path. In fact, as Moondi questioned the strangers through Gatti, the pale people had seemed very defensive, almost deliberately trying to avoid the enquiry. Then the atmosphere had suddenly become tense. Some of the Hupla warriors were all for finishing the matter there and then. Whatever story they were spinning, the pale ones had obviously meant to offend. It was quite blatant. They could quickly disarm the Dani opposition (who were themselves properly dressed) with a view to killing them all at a feast, and offering them to the bird-spirit when, and if, it returned.

Urgently Gatti had explained that the flapping, moving, vegetable drapes were really the pale people's equivalent of a gourd. They had many different drapes for different occasions—and Gatti had made them show how they could take them off and put them on, and how they could wear various other drapes which they had concealed in their opaque carrying bags (the Hupla carried everything in open-weave mesh bags) which they cleverly secured on their backs.

The pale people, Gatti concluded, were actually wearing the very best gourd-drapes they possessed—in good faith of a peaceable reception. And besides, he had added, the strangers knew all about the noisy flying spirit. To them it was familiar and friendly, and it would not be at all pleased with their sacrifice. In fact, he said, one of the things they particularly wanted was to arrange for it to become a regular visitor to the valley. It would bring many good things with it. And at that point he had shown them a knife.

Moondi had been captivated by the knife. He was shown what it could do, and was amazed. Even now it was amazing. But at the time he had scarcely believed it. And when one of the pale people had produced one from his sack, and gravely offered it to Moondi as 'a gift to the leader of the Hupla hunting party', he had lowered his bow, and commanded the escort to resume the trek forthwith. Of course he knew now that the so-called bird-spirit was in fact a winged carrier, used by the pale people for moving themselves and their things around. Though it was still a mystery quite how it all worked, it no longer seemed wild and unpredictable. And the pale people certainly did control it. And what it delivered. There was no doubt at all of that.

On arrival in the village the visitors had been led directly to his father's hut, and soon a solemn tribal meeting had been called. Moondi went along as of right, and heard Gatti tell of what at the time had been disturbing and strange things. Now, much later, he had learned to take these things for granted. Though he couldn't say he liked all of it even now.

Gatti told them that outside the valley there were many peoples. That much he had known, or at least suspected. There were even peoples who inhabited the lowlands. Wide watery plains, hot and humid, with vicious many-toothed wild animals and spiky, reedy plants, a few flat-topped trees and more verdant interlaced jungle canopy. It sounded a nightmare. Further away still there were vast stretches of water, and places where people lived with no trees at all. In these places many of the people were pale. And they were very powerful. And some of them . . . and here Gatti had paused, choosing his words carefully . . . some of them claimed to exercise controlling rights over the High Valleys and over the Hupla. They were led by the Distant Chief.

This threw the meeting into an uproar, and once again

the lives of the visitors seemed under immediate threat. But Gatti and the pale ones protested hotly that they had no relation to this Distant Chief. They were merely warning the Hupla that the Distant Chief was powerful, and might well have his warriors pay them a visit. It was all very unpleasant news. Up till then they had never seen anyone but Hupla, or possibly Dani, in the valley, and those who wanted to exercise rights over it generally came and called formal battles or, if devious, sung spell songs over it from a distance.

In the actual event, over the intervening years, the rule of the Distant Chief had proved... well... distant. Though in one significant instance it was indirectly effectual: word had come from the Dani some distance away that a battle called with the Yali (who not only killed their enemies but ate them too—a particularly direct, if uncouth, way of endorsing a victory Moondi had always thought) had been interrupted by the unexpected arrival of a small force of green warriors. They had been draped in what looked like textured leaves, and had made a considerable noise with short, flaming stabbing spears. Dani or Yali warriors who had attempted to rebuff this sacrilegious interruption had suddenly found themselves shockingly wounded with arrows they had not been able to see. After a very few moments it had been evident that the power of the green warriors was insuperable. One of them had then announced, with a loud rattling voice, in poor Dani, that battle was prohibited, and that they must return to their villages. They had realized there wasn't much choice.

From that time on, mused Moondi, offended Hupla, including himself, had curtailed their battles and raids quite considerably. The general impression was that the Distant Chief would soon know if and when a battle was called, and would send in his green warriors to stop it. There were other reasons, too, why fighting was less popular among the Hupla. Reasons connected with the

89

arrival of the pale people in the valley, two of whom were now living there permanently. A man and his wife.

In all, though, the Distant Chief contented himself with appointing one of their number as Tribal Representative—Kwalogo, Moondi's younger brother. Kwalogo had walked out of the village alone one day, and had returned many days later with a piece of paper and a woven collar to indicate his new status. For this he had not been popular. Apart from anything else he was Moondi's younger brother, and had no rights to power within the tribe. Moondi was being groomed to take over as High Elder, not Kwalogo. And for another thing he was almost entirely self-centred. Before a feast he was the last to offer a pig for the celebration. But he, or one of his wives, was always the first at Moondi's door invoking 'family' if there was a surplus of sweet potatoes on Moondi's land. He was first there also if he needed a hand for hut repairs. But reciprocal requests from Moondi, or his other brothers, always seemed to come 'just at a difficult time'. And Kwalogo was the last to volunteer to go hunting if the expedition looked if it would be away long, or threatened unusual exertion or danger. Kwalogo would never have run across Dani expeditions in the forest. A fact which, taking into consideration his hiking out alone, pointed to the significance he had obviously attached to becoming tribal representative. He never actually refused to do any of his tribal duties, but he seemed to do them when it suited *him* rather than the tribe—and this was not the attitude encouraged in a potential Elder.

It was knowing his brother that caused Moondi a little concern about the pig. It was not his brother's pig that was being sent out of the valley. And he wondered about that. In the circumstances he would have expected Kwalogo to jump in first. He was the one who had introduced the scheme to the valley, at the Distant Chief's request. And he was always keen on anything that offered trading discs. In particular he had taken the lead—though not so much of the work—under Gatti, the bubbly Dani, when the landing ground had been built.

The Hupla Elders had deliberated long and hard when the strangers had mentioned a landing ground for their winged carrier. Two of the pale people wanted to stay— with the Hupla's permission—in the valley, they had said. But they needed material and equipment to live there. And most of this would be brought for them by the carriers, as well as the durables that the Hupla might want. The Elders were undecided, fearing much that was nameless. True, the Dani with the strangers had offered assurances, but it was a significant and irrevocable step. In the end, what had decided them was the result of a Healing Day when the strangers had inspected each tribesman in turn, and then given them little beans to eat or small pricks on the arm. Gatti had assured them this was normal, and very soon healing of many things would take place—without Spirit Talkers or dances or life sacrifices or personal butchery at the Table of Hands. So it had proved.

The pale people had great powers and, as Gatti had promised, ailments which had beset the Hupla, some for as long as they could remember, began to disappear: gross, running skin growths and racking bloody coughs, and even the sleeping fever that had claimed the lives of so many children before the last battle.

No more than thirty days later they had started to clear a section of the valley, under the direction of the experienced Dani, to accept the winged carrier. It was hard back-breaking work, but they were awarded discs for it— and all the landing ground workers could sport personal knives in proof of their service.

Proud and glorious had been the day when the first tiny speck on the skyline had grown, buzzing like a determined bee, into the roaring eagle they had once so much feared. The winged carrier swept magnificently down into the valley, crunching down on the cleared brown-baked ground, growling and whining, and wobbling its stiff wings, and throwing up clouds of dust as it coasted to a halt in front of the enthusiastic tribesmen. It looked to Moondi more like a startled insect than a bird, he thought. Spidery and angular, with a big belly.

The carrier's minder had stepped out and smiled and shaken everyone by the hand (it was their custom—which the Hupla had now adopted, when meeting them), and then pulled a wonderful collection of durables, including beautifully fashioned bright-stone pots for cooking, out of the carrier's belly. These were mostly for the pale residents' new wooden home, but some were for the Hupla as a 'thank you'. It had been a most memorable day.

And today would certainly be another memorable day. Today Moondi's carefully prepared and wrapped meat would be speeding off in that same belly very shortly. He paused and looked over to the cleft in the ridge that was the sighting point for arriving carriers. He listened. Normally the distant bee-like drone, rising and falling, was the sound which announced its approach. But the only sound at present was the cackle of birds, and the sound of Folukwe and Mu-lew working in the garden hoeing the sweet crop. And the wind in the jungle tree-tops. The only flying objects were the darting blue butterflies which haunted the flowers of the forest.

Dukwe looked up. He had stopped passing her meat. The job was done. Carefully he drew the bloody bones and head together, and deposited them in a mesh bag. Dukwe did the same with the wrapped meat.

Where *was* the carrier? He looked again, the length of the valley. Cloud was beginning to rise, earlier than usual, and darker. Rain would be early today he concluded. He went inside the hut and carefully replaced his working gourd with one more fitting to the occasion, plumed, but not his best. Appropriate. Then he hoisted the packaged meat over his shoulder, and strode down to the pale ones' wooden home near the strip. He would wait for it there.

As he approached he could hear the man talking to himself. Well not to himself, but not to his wife either, who was out holding a healing meeting further up the valley. He was actually talking into the Sounding Chest which crackled and hissed and gabbled all day in the corner of his room. Moondi knew he used it to talk to other people in other valleys—and to the carriers' minders when they were flying. It was very powerful and very mysterious, and almost certainly spiritual and dangerous. Most importantly, though, it was the source of the pale man's apparently inexhaustible supplies.

Moondi paused at the doorway. Gra-Ham, the man, turned at his approach. His face was serious.

'Moondi,' he spoke carefully in the Hupla language which had taken him so long to master, 'I really am very sorry, but the winged carrier has said he cannot come today. He cannot find his way into the valley. The clouds are here too early.'

Moondi stared.

'But I have killed the pig!' he exclaimed loudly. 'He *must* come!'

'He cannot, Moondi. He just cannot. He would be risking his life to try. He will try to come soon. In three or four days.' Moondi shook his head. He could not see how clouds could be dangerous. He had walked often in clouds along the high ridges. There was nothing to fear.

'He *must* come!' he repeated. 'Later will be too late. The meat will not be good.' Everyone knew that. 'Tell him he must come!' he shouted again, almost spitting in anger.

'No Moondi, it is not possible. He knows what is safe, and he has decided. I'm really very sorry.'

'What can I do with all this meat then, Gra-Ham? It's for trading. You know it's for trading. It has to go on the carrier!'

'You will have to eat it here, Moondi. I *am* sorry. I cannot help the clouds. It just happens like that sometimes.'

Moondi was unconvinced. Was it a trick? Was the pale man tricking him? He did not seem to be. But these were different people. Who knew what they were thinking—or planning? He tried a test to watch his reaction.

'Then we must all eat the meat tomorrow, Gra-Ham?'

'I suppose you'll have to,' he commented sadly. He did seem to want to help. 'I tell you what. You call a feast for your family, and I'll come up and tell some more of my stories. How will that do?' Then he added quickly, as if sensing Moondi had lead him on deliberately, 'I'll come up *after* you have all eaten.'

Moondi grunted his assent. At least it did not seem Gra-Ham had stopped the carrier himself, in order to eat a pig. But he was not pleased. Unfaithful winged carrier. He'd prepared everything so particularly too. He couldn't credit it. The very first time. It was afraid of clouds! Now he was faced with the double embarrassment of offering hospitality at very short notice with the meat wrongly butchered, and the fire down so low it would be fortunate if he could heat enough stones to cook it overnight at all. And everyone in the village would know about it in the time it took him to walk home.

Then he thought of his brother. His little greedy eyes would light up at the thought of a family feast—on a pig from Moondi's stock. No wonder he hadn't offered his own pig for the trade! He knew all about the scheme, and obviously knew the carriers didn't always come to collect. Moondi grunted angrily and loudly as he paced back up to his hut. That brother of his had it coming to him. Then he had a thought, worthy of an Elder. He would make sure that Kwalogo got a really horrible, firm meaty piece tonight. He would casually explain that he couldn't help it. It had been cut for trading—not for his much respected family. His brother, of all people, must surely understand these constraints? Yes, that would do it.

Moondi brightened visibly at the prospect.

10
Love

Moondi sat comfortably by the blazing fire, his face and chest hot and red in the fierce flickering light, his back cool, but not cold, his stomach full of juicy pork and sweet potatoes, pleasurably distended against his gourd. What a meal! Good food certainly put unfaithful carriers in a different light. They had finished eating their meal late. The sun had set many hours ago, for it had been a rush to cook the meat—or rather to find the time to let it cook properly. But they had managed it.

First the great fire had been built up by the family working together, stacking it up with logs and branches which they had been drying for their own fires. Among these blazing embers, the women had placed the best and squarest of the large cooking stones they kept by the huts. These stayed in the heart of the fire until judged hot enough by the cooks to be carefully and precariously extracted, with a freshly split branch, glowing brightly in the now fast-falling darkness.

In the meantime a large pit had been dug in the brown soil, and lined with banana leaves. Then the bed of the trench had been immediately paved with heated stones. The meat, wrapped in banana leaves, was placed on top of these, along with vegetables—most importantly sweet potatoes—and the lining leaves brought over, and secured across the meal. Finally the cooking started. Much later, when the sun had crept down below the ridge, the cooks had deemed the meat sufficiently baked, and had exhumed it, steaming, from the cooking pit to be handed out to the waiting family. Moondi was sure to choose the right one for his brother. The effect was as predicted. He was delighted to see him chew violently on the meaty portion apologetically left for him by Dukwe. And half-way through the meal Moondi had smiled blandly, and commented that butchering meat carefully for market was a particular and unusual skill which he had perfected, and that he apologized if anyone had not had their usual cut or portion on this occasion. He hoped they understood.

Protests came back from the family that he wasn't to worry; the meat was rich, fatty and succulent. Excellent, in fact—which it was, for it was a prime pig he had killed. It was a clever skill, they said. Next time he was sure to get it to market on the carrier. The only one who declined to comment was Kwalogo, his brother. Then his silence made him obvious, so he too offered his condolences as to the loss of trade. Moondi enjoyed the rest of the party.

Gra-Ham joined them, as promised, later on. Out of courtesy he accepted a sweet potato, but no pork. Moondi was looking forward to his coming. Gra-Ham was good at telling stories. Stories that he got out of The Book. A book was a durable that had been a complete mystery to the Hupla. They did not know what it was made of, though now they knew it was wood, like the bark from a tree, but they could not make out what it was used for. It took some time to realize that it contained information which the pale people valued. He had had it explained to him once rather as the Hupla would leave signs in the jungle for other warriors to see and understand. Indications as to which trail they had taken, their success on the hunt, and so on. These had been drummed into Moondi as a boy, and he had practised both making and reading them until he knew them instinctively. Now, an experienced hunter could even know by the style of the signs—broken twigs, blazes on trees, and so on—which warrior from a hunting-party had made them. Books were similar. Full of marks and signs. And The Book was special. That was because it was the book of the Great Spirit.

For some time after Gra-Ham and his wife, the Healer, had come to stay in the valley (the first strangers had left some time ago) there was wide speculation as to what he was doing there. Was he from the Distant Chief (though he insisted not), and keeping an eye on them? Was he singing a complex and sinister spell on them all, with the assistance of the carrier? This seemed unlikely. The one or two Dani who came too explained that neither the carrier nor the pale people were involved in spells. Quite the reverse. They had come, as had the Dani with them, to show why spell songs and divinations which called for the bloody and heart-rending sacrifice of their children, the mutilation of their wives, and continual reprisal battles and raids were not the real or necessary way of life for a noble people of the High Valleys.

Indeed, the Dani had found a better way. This they had explained on a number of occasions at large meetings in the villages of the valley. And many had listened. The tall, now serious-faced Dani explained how they had been taught the stories of The Book, stories of a far-away tribe that had been chosen for unique contact with the Great Spirit, and how they had, through many problems, come to understand something of him and his great dealings. Despite this, the final communication from the Great One, in the form of a God-Human, the tribe had killed in ignorance and distrust. But he, being of the Great One, had come back to life.

The Dani explained that the Spirit of this restored God-Human was all one with the Great Spirit, and now met and dealt with men and women one-to-one, not with tribes. Because he had lived as a human, he understood and sympathized with each one. He did not demand sacrifices; he did not demand fingers; his only war was against those who did. His coming, when intimately accepted, brought peace in the heart, and a freedom from the great oppression of the spirits which—as Dani and Hupla acknowledged alike—weighed on them continually.

It was strong and complex stuff. And it contained one element that Moondi disliked and distrusted. Much was made of the idea of Love. This he did not, he was sure he could not, understand. It was the key to this new thinking which had captured the hearts, he knew, of many people in the valley already. Meetings and gatherings happened regularly now, centred on stories from The Book, about the God-Human, Jesus, and his sayings and ideas. But Moondi didn't go along. He liked the stories. They were sparkling and attractive and true to life, with odd twists in the tail.

Moondi himself was a good teller of stories. His hope for Eldership in the village was based as much on his ability to speak well and wisely, as on his hunting and fighting ability, or the patronage of his father. But he was afraid of being tricked. Caught up in something that was not right. Right by his tribe, and right by his nature. It was attractive, possibly true. By all accounts The Book was authentic. But love? What was that, and why should it matter so much to the Great One? Where came duty, respect, tribal loyalty, tribal tradition, and self-preservation? Were these all to be sacrificed? For him it was impossible. But he liked the stories. And, like the Dani 'Christians'—as they called themselves—Gra-Ham was good at telling stories.

Moondi had to admit that the Christians, pale or otherwise, had brought much that was good into the valley. There was great healing which, under the direction of Gra-Ham's wife, went on now day by day in an amazing way. Durables had come—which halved the workload of so many tasks. And even, he suspected, they affected the influence of the Distant Chief—the 'Government of Indonesia'. Moondi's brother, the Tribal

Representative, had mentioned a number of projects suggested to him by the government—one of them was the removal of gourds from all the tribesmen in the valleys!

This sort of thing the Christians had quietly defused, or rejected, as impractical or invasive of the tribal culture. Yes, they were good people—and this 'love' they had spoken of must be very potent.

For he knew that Dani liked to live and work in Dani country, not Hupla country. They liked to be at home. However, for the sake of this message, this thinking, this service of the Great One God, the Dani had left home to trek across the valleys. He felt, rather than knew, that the same might apply to the pale people too. They had no need to come to bring healing, or carriers, to the valley. It was nothing to them. And yet it was. Everything. They said they really had no choice. God, who 'loved' them, wanted them to 'love' the Hupla. There was that inexplicable word again.

The firelight warmed and comforted Moondi, and he relaxed, letting go of the conundrum. With the comfort of good food, and the intriguing lilt of the pale man's accent (so different even from a Dani speaking Hupla), he was drawn into the story. It was a story about a wandering Hupla.

Gra-Ham's eye sparkled as he told it, adding little touches to the tale as it unfolded, his face and eyes hardening and softening, as rigid or gentle attitudes expressed themselves in the tale. His voice just carried over the low crackling of the partly-spent fire and the background of night jungle sounds.

'A Hupla went on a journey one day,' he began, 'down to the tribes of a distant valley, many days' walk along the jungle trail. And as he came to a dark and difficult part of the route he was suddenly ambushed, and gravely wounded by a band of renegade warriors who had been turned out of their tribe for stealing pigs. He lay on the path for a long time until by chance there came another Hupla, making the same journey. This man was a warrior, a proud and noble warrior, a man of the forest and of the chase. A man of tribal ambition, even the son of a High Elder.'

At this point Moondi felt a particular interest in the story. 'But,' continued Gra-Ham, 'when he saw the wounded man on the jungle trail he immediately suspected a further ambush, for he knew the raiders must be near and desperate, so he slipped quickly into the undergrowth, and worked his way around the man, by silent and skilful field-craft, back to the trail at a safe distance further along.'

Moondi felt, on balance, that this had not been such a bad idea. But if he had been the wounded man he would have hoped, perhaps, that a confederate of the High Valleys would have taken more risks, and shown some concern over him.

'Next along the jungle path—for it was a busy and much used route—came a Hupla Spirit Talker, one whose job it was to define the patterns of his village life, to whom the loss of a warrior would be highly significant and, above all, a man who knew something of healing.'

Moondi could see quickly that here was a far more appropriate rescuer. What did a warrior know of healing compared with a Talker?

'But the Talker was not so sure that the omens were right for a healing that morning when he saw the hurt body slumped against the tree-stump across the narrow path. The spirits of his valley were perhaps too distant to help. The location hardly propitious, and the essential personal knowledge as to who had done the wounding, and why, was missing. The Talker, regretfully, though not without a certain concern for his person, took another path through the bush, as the warrior had. He muttered a few verses of a healing song, at a distance, before he went on.'

Moondi now was disgruntled. Two of the obvious possible sources of help had been dismissed. Perhaps the man would be left to die—and his spirit would rise to haunt them all. That would be a good ending.

'Then along the trail came a Yali.'

Moondi coughed out loud. This was going to be a massacre. The Yali would dispatch him—and then eat him on the spot, most likely. The Yali were not personable people. Not to the Hupla.

'The Yali took pity on the wounded warrior, and picked soft leaves to bind his wounds, offered him water to drink which he carried from a nearby stream, and made a carrying pallet out of tree branches and grass, and secured the warrior on to it as comfortably as he could. Then, tying the branches to his waist, he transported him to the next village which was half a day's walk on the narrow track. When he got there he asked a man he knew to open his hut to the patient, and to get his wives to care for him until his health was restored. As payment he left part of his sack of sweet potatoes. Saying "If you feel the obligation is greater, I will give you more on my return."

'Now,' said Gra-Ham, looking around. 'A question. Who was friend to the man who was wounded?'

Moondi had been surprised by the turn of the story but could see the point clearly enough. The man's tribal compatriots—from whom help should have come, been expected, even—had ignored him. The enemy tribesman had proved the most honourable.

'The Yali,' he offered from the circle around the fire.

'And why do you suppose that was?' said Gra-Ham.

Moondi thought. 'He was a man of wide compassion—a wise man perhaps. A man to whom tribal loyalties were less important,' he hazarded.

'Certainly all of those, Moondi. Very much all of those. But when Jesus told the story, or one very like it, he was pointing out that the man who stopped was the man who *loved*.'

101

Moondi coughed again. He should have known it. Jesus and love. It always seemed to come down to them. Gra-Ham was the man of The Book, and that was what the book was about. It just spoiled a good story to keep coming back to it.

'Moondi, I know you don't want to talk about Jesus, but it seems strange to me that you never want to talk about love either,' said Gra-Ham suddenly.

Moondi looked startled. Something in the way he had spoken had stirred his heart. Perhaps because it had been put so directly. No, he did not know what 'love' was. None of his family did either, as far as he could tell. In conversation after conversation with the Dani—who could explain most things in their extrovert manner—and with Gra-Ham, he had never really seen the point. He did not want to talk about it because he did not understand it. But was he also afraid of it?

'Yes, Gra-Ham, he "loved" him, you say. But this "love"—it used him. Didn't it? It used his strength—he had to carry him all that way on the pallet. That must have made him tired and sore at best. It hurt him. Then it made him use up his trade produce to make sure the warrior was cared for. He even offered more! That was a great cost. "Love" is not a useful thing, Gra-Ham.'

Moondi could see Gra-Ham sigh. He was sorry for that because he enjoyed his stories, and he knew that Gra-Ham knew this love to be important. He wanted to find it. If only for Gra-Ham's sake. If only to know why it pulled so strongly. Then he could choose to take it or leave it.

Two logs, stacked up and supporting each other in the fire, had burnt through. Suddenly they collapsed inwards sending a shower of swirling sparks funnelling up into the now cloudless night sky. Little sparky spirits, he thought, each jostling for position, like flies around a piece of putrid meat. They didn't care if one was injured or could not feed. As long as they got their own fill. He looked across at Gra-Ham whose features were briefly more visible in the bright flare of light. His eyes were closed, and he seemed to be murmuring to himself. Moondi was surprised. He had thought he was looking at him as he spoke. He felt, rather than knew, that he was doing something spiritual. Something that involved the conversation they were having.

Gra-Ham looked up. 'Moondi, I don't know why I feel I should say this, but I will.' He paused. 'My wife and I. We have "love" for each other. In my country . . .' as he said these words a touch of sad softness came into his voice, and Moondi saw in a flash of insight that Gra-Ham missed his own homeland deeply. 'Back home in my country, my valley, young men and women usually expect to discover "love" between each other before they are married.'

A strange feeling came over Moondi as he heard those words. It was as though they had been meant just for him—which in a sense they had. But it was more than that, it was as though Gra-Ham had known, or had been told, that he of all people would understand them. And the truth was, he did. Or was beginning to. As Gra-Ham had spoken of his wife, and 'love', and young men and women discovering 'love', and as he had shown on his face a deep longing for the valley of his own people, a rich mixture of emotions began to stir in Moondi's heart—and in his soul. He understood how someone could long for their home valley.

And he understood by a leap of intuition that the longing he had felt that morning when he had thought of Lanya for the first time for many seasons was very, very similar. Not only that, but it was a longing which melted the heart; it was a longing that actually hurt, though it was something he would not be without. It was a feeling it was right to have. Good to have. Important for him, Moondi, to have, to be himself. But, oh, it cost. It hurt to have it.

Was this, he dared ask himself, was this something like 'love'? He got up from his comfortable position by the fire, and walked around the circle of his friends and relatives to where Gra-Ham sat, still, on the ground, but eyes open now. Expectant, though in the background of his gaze there was still the sorrow of deserted valleys. Valleys of home.

'Is the God of "love" someone who touches your soul with longing, Gra-Ham? Beautiful, but painful longing?'

Moondi was no longer aware of the fire, or of the tribesmen around it. He was not aware of the background chatter of the women, nor the desultory grunt of pigs, nor the more distant animal sounds of the jungle valley at night. He could only see those steady gentle eyes. And through them the eyes of her, she of his youth. The one who should have been no more to him than her bride-price of pigs, but had shown him, in her life and in her death, the first steps down a trail which led into a vast and magnificent valley, towering deep and wide with a lush green canopy, a valley of the soul in which he never, until now, knew he could walk, nor suspected even existed before this night.

Gra-Ham reached out, and without a word clasped him to him. Moondi let out a sound that was a mixture between a cry of joy and a sob of anguish.

'Oh, yes, Moondi. Yes, yes. That is love. That *is* love!'

11
Moving On

I had been in the army now for eight years. Four years with the paras, and four in an Army Air Corps squadron at Wildenrath in (then) West Germany.

After the paras, flying in Germany had been rather pedestrian—VIP flying and 'general duties', which usually meant more VIP flying. Then there was the odd medical 'casevac'. But at least it had been the sort of posting that included 'home'. In fact, home had featured enough for us to start a family. Already our first baby—little Sarah—was growing up, and baby Nicola wasn't far behind. What was also good was that Mary had settled into army life much more too. And so had I.

Cold war soldiering perhaps hadn't the thrill of active operations in Northern Ireland, but it was comfortable and familiar, well paid and well planned. Perhaps, I thought, I should sign on for a further term. Promotion was due, given a pass in the—quite straightforward—exams. My Christian faith was a satisfying and, I believed, significant part of my work as an officer with the men under my command. No doubt: to continue in the army offered a worthwhile career. But at the back of my mind I knew that I had joined up from very different motives. Suddenly I was at a key point in my life, and the future was something I needed to think about very seriously indeed. But I did get one last fling at military adventure, though much of it I can't really talk about even today. I went to work for the SAS.

Word got around that our Hereford Heroes were in need of a specialist helicopter pilot. I showed interest, and once again found myself up before the Brigadier.

'Well, Marfleet. Looks like you're the sort of idiot they need to do this job,' he opened cordially.

'Thank you, sir. What does it involve?'

'I'm afraid I can't tell you.'

'Right, sir. I see. When do I start?'

'I have no idea. Soon, I expect.'

'Thank you, sir. Will it be a UK posting?'

'Might be. Might not. Might be anywhere. Wherever it is, whatever it is, you won't be able tell anyone, not even Mary. All classified. Clear?' he ended.

Recalling our relative ranks I avoided commenting that it would be quite hard to be absolutely clear on all the details. The interview concluded in a similar vein.

'How will I know if I've got the job, sir?'

'You won't. Just be ready to go, that's all.'

'Yes, sir. Thank you for your help sir.'

By now I had got the feeling that, whatever it was I had to do, it was all pretty secret. Army training gives you these perceptive insights. That and broad military experience. For several days afterwards I resisted the temptation to stop and question anyone I saw in a high-collared raincoat, slouch hat, and chain-smoking unlit cigarettes. I was rewarded by receiving a simple telephone call from the CO's office which indicated I was to fly to 22 SAS Regiment in Hereford forthwith. This I did, collecting a Scout for the purpose, and found myself assigned as the only pilot attached to a brand new elite SAS unit set up under the express orders of the Home Secretary. It was to be called the (Secret) Anti-terrorist Squad.

This specialist squad was to burst into public consciousness by the spectacular way they ended the Iranian Embassy siege in London in 1980. But at the start, and even today, in much of what they do they remain deliberately in the shadows.

I was told to shed my uniform, and, in the style of the times, grow my hair long, and buy in a varied range of flared jeans and floral shirts. Man, I was one cool pilot. I was to be on call twenty-four hours a day—so I couldn't take a drink—and, as the Brigadier had accurately informed me, when I went home occasionally on a day's leave, I couldn't tell Mary what it was all about. Which was pretty strange for her, especially when the regulation green army flying suit was left hanging in the wardrobe, and various shades of designer jeans regularly appeared in need of the ironing board. It also made 'shop' talk at home rather one-sided. But, as she said, who wanted to talk about the army anyway?

Much of my flying time was, of necessity, training and practice. In those early days it was all quick response exercises and detailed evaluation of the 'threat'. We would think up possible incidents, and then decide how we would deal with them. Then we would try it all out to see if it worked. If not, then . . . back to the drawing board. Very quick response was always the key.

Perhaps we would be sitting peacefully in a Herefordshire pub (myself deeply into fizzy lemonade) when suddenly all the alert bleepers would go off at once. Chirping like a flock of hungry sparrows we'd eject from the bar at the rush, leaving the landlord to think it was something that he'd said, and hit the road down to HQ. There we'd be briefed. An aircraft had been 'hijacked' or a politician 'kidnapped', and the problem would be sitting on a nearby deserted MOD site waiting for us to go in and sort it out.

The day would inevitably end with lots of bangs and fireworks, and self hovering menacingly over the 'hijacked' plane or 'hostage building' while black-suited action men, minus chocolates but carrying just about everything else, slid urgently down dangling ropes on to wings, tails or roofs, and proceeded to blast noisily into passenger cabins or upstairs rooms. All exciting stuff. And, as I have said before, the SAS were certainly impressive. Working in small tight-knit groups they were very informal and very individual—for an army unit—and always in deadly earnest. Like the Pony Express, they always got through. And, as their pilot, I was expected to do so too.

I remember a call one night. I was bleeped to get to Heathrow in a hurry. (There was never any other speed.) I bundled out of bed, and pulled on my jeans and bomber jacket, and, the REME ground crew having pre-flighted the aircraft, I dashed off across Hereford to pick up the CO from his home in a village outside (Colonel Peter de la Billiere at the time, as it happens). As I flew over the quiet rural hamlet a neat illuminated landing 'T' flashed up at me from the ground. His family were all up out of bed on the croquet lawn, armed with torches to bring me in!

He clambered aboard, and I quickly slid back to HQ so he could collect the relevant equipment. By then the depot was silent. The flurry of activity which had accompanied my departure had subsided. 'The boys' were already on their way scorching down the M4 in their turbo-charged 3.8 litre Rangerovers. The blue-light police escort doing its best to keep up.

I took off again, and set course east. As part of the anti-terrorist operation, I had been given a priority call-sign which, when uttered, was supposed to stop the air traffic controllers in mid-sentence, make them drop their coffee, ignore their still-burning cigarettes, and offer me their undivided attention. In reality, though, this rather depended on how well read they were, operationally.

Just east of Gloucester I came across a problem: 'Brize Norton, this is Army Three Seven Seven. Request zone transit to Heathrow Approach. Priority COAL SCUTTLE. Over.'

'Army Three Seven Seven, this is Brize. Ah, negative. I have continuous conflicting heavy-jet traffic engaged in exercise WATER MELON. Re-route south via Swindon, over.'

'Brize, this is Three Seven Seven. I say again, priority COAL SCUTTLE. Over.'

'Three Seven Seven, what means COAL SCUTTLE? Over.'

'Brize, this is Army Three Seven Seven. I am at 2,000 feet on course One One Five, overhead Burford, and *coming on through*. Refer to your Operations Manual or *get the Air Marshall out of bed and ask him!* I don't mind which. Three Seven Seven, out.'

We touched skids at Heathrow without further delay. To be met by the Guards Captain, the SAS team leader, who jumped smartly out of the back of his Rangerover, acknowledging, but not saluting, his superior. What had kept us? He asked with a smile.

As I said, they only ever moved at one speed.

Another thing we practised was HALO drops. High Altitude, Low Opening. Free fall parachuting. The parachute is opened by a barometric device operated by air pressure at a certain height. This was the method used to infiltrate the SAS into the Falkland Islands ahead of the landings during Operation Corporate. It avoids risking the aircraft at low level, and enemy observers do not suspect paratroops.

I was delivering a four man stick from the Scout. We had climbed to the jump height of 10,000 feet, and I gave the signal. There was a scrabble and thump as the men flung themselves over the side. As usual, I looked down to count the helmets to check all had gone safely. I could see only three. Alarmed I went into a steep spiral dive. What had gone wrong? Still only three. Thoroughly concerned now I was startled to receive a sharp and desperate tap on my shoulder. Number four was still on board!

For the last minute he had been valiantly battling for *our* lives just behind me. His barometric device had triggered, and spilled his chute out all over the rear cockpit. Sucked out of the rear door into the slip-stream it had been waving around like a gigantic flag within inches of my tail-rotor. Unsecured and down on his knees the poor soldier had desperately pulled his errant chute back into the aircraft (before it killed us both) while I was executing my violent manoeuvres. Only then had he been able to crawl over to alert me. It had been a very close thing. A helicopter with an entangled tail rotor is finished.

In Germany, by comparison, life was much more conventional, and although there were occasionally one or two urgent medical cases the adrenalin pumped less often as the flying settled into a very regular and comfortable routine. But I—we—had a decision to take. Reference 'upwards' being the rule in the Christian's life, as well as in the army, I prayed very specially for some answers. They weren't long in coming.

To stay in the army I would have to be promoted to Major. It was certainly about time, and the exams I would be required to pass were pretty straightforward. It should be a doddle. I had a good record, especially in Germany where I had earned a reputation as a cheerful and safe VIP pilot. The Colonels and Generals liked the idea of being ferried around by a proper para, and I made sure I was always turned out better and arrived more promptly than the rest. I might not like VIP flying much, but I was determined to be the very best they had. That was the business of being a soldier. I decided to go ahead with my exams.

Not long after, the phone rang.

'David, where were you yesterday?'

'Yesterday?'

'Yes, promotion exams . . .'

'*Yesterday*?!'

I had forgotten the date. Unbelievable. I never, never miss dates. Not only that, but the whole of an officer's life revolves around organization and timing. The work of any manager is the same. I had achieved the impossible. Falling at the first post without even starting the race!

That week I was to take a V-VIP flight. I had to take the Commander-In-Chief, British Army Of the Rhine, Mr Especially-Big himself (General Sir Harry Tuzo), to a NATO planning meeting. Take off, 08 30hrs. Now as I said, VIP flights are expected to be on the button. For V-VIP flights they want the button polished. As the second hand comes up to the chosen minute those skids touch the deck, and so on. Pilot has shiny helmet, pressed flying suit, glowing boots, the works. It forms part of the boss's image. Especially in NATO. Foreigners to impress. High class chauffeur with wings.

That morning I overslept.

So did Mary.

My flying suit was in the wash.

I missed the weather briefing.

All in all, it was not my morning. I was saved from complete disgrace by my ground crew who got the machine ready for me (while I was battling with the traffic), and the General, who exercised his V-VIP right to be late.

Unbelievable. I *don't* oversleep.

I believed I was getting the message.

I decided to drop around to see a very faithful Christian colleague on the base—Major Graeme Halliburton, a Squadron Commander in the Royal Signals. He laughed when I told him of my prayers, and what had happened since.

'I'm sorry to say you are probably right if you think God is telling you something. He does rather have that sort of humour. "He's no respecter of persons," it says in the Bible!'

I ruefully agreed.

'Not only that,' he continued. 'God doesn't keep changing his mind all the time. If you feel you joined the army with such a specific purpose, then I'd be

111

surprised if he didn't want you to stick to it.'

We prayed together, and I left with a lighter heart. Later in the evening Mary and I had a long discussion. She said that she too, as she had prayed, had begun to feel perhaps that the time *had* come to say goodbye to one service, and take up the burden of another.

In the spring of 1979, at the end of my eight-year commission, I declined to extend it. Our calling, we believed, lay elsewhere.

12
California

The tiny airstrip carved out of the Colorado Desert looked every bit as welcoming as the cemetery in Tombstone Gulch. It also bore a more than passing resemblance. Bounded by grey slab-like rocks, and set in a dry, dusty, desolate valley floor it was just twenty minutes' flying time in a Cessna 185 mission training aircraft out of Redlands, the Mission Aviation Fellowship US HQ, in southern California. Yes, that's right. Where it never rains. I could certainly vouch for that. It was a dry and arid part of the globe. And just at that moment my mouth was as dry as the desert I was flying over.

My Texan instructor had just laconically pointed out the diminutive slash in the yellow wasteland below as a practice airstrip, mission class 'C'. And would I care to try it. Class 'C' meant it came about mid-range in the hazard stakes when classifying dangerous air termini. 'C' demanded a higher degree of skill on landing than 'A' or 'B' (which to my mind were quite bad enough, being roughly the equivalent of crumpled postage stamps with and without the perforations, respectively). It was not as bad as 'D' and 'E', which offered additional challenges by way of dead-end stops at cliff faces, or twenty per cent slopes down (or up) on touchdown. At least on this one I could go around again if I missed. Actually, I would probably have to go around again even if I didn't. But one thing at a time.

The instructor was, I knew by now, somewhat short on words of advice. It comes from a heritage of long nights alone on the range, I expect. But if he thought I could do it, well, no doubt he would mention if he thought I was missing something. 'In for a dime, in for a dollar,' I said to myself philosophically as I dropped towards the strip. You see, not at all bad. The local language classes were coming along. Sure thing.

As I sunk towards the desert he casually added that a 'C' class strip might also have a 'lil' ole rock or rooted lumber sittin' down the-ar' meaning that somewhere along its length there might be an obstruction, and would I mind simulating this by trying a wing lift during the landing roll. Now, it would be untrue to say that I didn't know how this was done. I just didn't think I was quite ready to try it yet. Certainly as I was having doubts about making the strip at all. But he was the trail boss.

'Now y'all just put her down, like a' showed ya,' he murmured, tipping his Stetson back, and putting his boots up on the instrument panel. He wasn't wearing either, and he didn't actually move, but I understood the intention of his spirit. Cultural orientation was coming along just fine too.

I concentrated on the cemetery, and endeavoured to oblige, bringing the near end of the narrow cart track into the centre of the windscreen, just over the nose through the spinning arc of the single propeller.

''Ere, Dave. You sure not thinnin' of going straight in, there?'

I grunted in recognition of his hint. I had forgotten. In mission flying a strip must always be 'dragged' first. By this stage it should have been second nature to me. Giving the strip a once-over before you went in to land. Going down as low as you can, and running the whole length, taking a good look. Sometimes it has to be from two or three thousand feet if the approach is awkward, but normally you go over much lower.

You check for animals or people on the runway, logs, cooking pots—anything left about, standing water, puddles, grass length, and so on. Only if it is clear to your satisfaction can you try to land. It's mandatory because it's a life-saver. And I had forgotten. I knew this would just be one more unpleasant day in a so far unpleasant course.

We had actually been 'accepted' as a family some months before by the British Mission Aviation Fellowship who had felt, despite my almost exclusive experience on helicopters, I was the right sort of pilot for them. More importantly, they confirmed that we did have a 'calling' to this work in a spiritual sense. They—the 'evaluation board'—had met us, and subjected us to a searching two week 'candidacy' course, after which they agreed there was some work for us to do with MAF, and asked us to consider joining.

Some might be surprised that either we or they needed such an assurance. Not many pilots volunteer for uncomfortable unpaid active service, with wife and family, in the primitive extremities of the world. All the more reason to be sure that those who do are soundly motivated, and have the resilience to stick it. Many, many times in the years to come we both needed to fall back on that assurance: that we were in the right business not only because *we* had felt 'called' to it, but because others, experienced Christian pilots, MAF board members, personal friends and supporters, had all tested our calling—and us—before offering their affirmation.

It had been a long road even before we got as far as candidacy. A welter of checks and flying exams in the UK and US, to translate my military experience into civilian licences, and then a full year of theological study at a Bible College in Hertfordshire—for both Mary and myself—our two little girls attending the creche provided. The course was regarded by MAF as crucial. I could see why.

115

It was to do with the essential nature of the job, similar in a way to army aviation: soldier first and then pilot.

Once assigned to a country I would be there to fly for the local church, local workers and evangelists, expatriate missionaries and, occasionally, government officials. But we would also be missionaries in our own right. We both needed to know our business properly—and the Bible, the basic textbook of our faith—to be qualified to understand and properly help those we were trying to serve.

But the base line, call or no call, was that I still had very little experience of fixed-wing flying—which was all the flying British MAF did. What then could I honestly expect to bring to this skilled and highly specific Christian outfit, even if I joined?

The thousands of hours I had as a pilot were certainly valuable. But for MAF? I needed those hours on the sort of aircraft I had so accurately identified as a teenager: rugged, single-engine, high-wing monoplanes.

Now, I may be many things, but I am not a simpleton. The real world makes real demands. No way could any of us expect to see those helicopter hours in my log-book suddenly transmute into fixed-wing experience. Whatever our supplementary use as a family, to be of any real value out there—with MAF—my contribution had to be as a rotary-winged pilot. By now it was on our minds to work perhaps in a mission elsewhere.

During this time I was asked to go to collect some delegates to an international MAF conference (there are seventeen nations and 140 planes involved in this operation) from Heathrow. So, as duty driver, I returned across the rolling countryside of southern England carrying some American colleagues to the conference venue in Kent. As I drove I fell to talking with one delegate who told me he was the Area Director of US MAF Operations in South-east Asia. He told me about a place called West Irian, recently re-named Irian Jaya. Out of courtesy I asked where it was. He replied that it was not far from

Borneo, north of Australia and, politically, part of Indonesia. I nodded, conversationally. Then he added something that nearly added us all to the motoring death statistics.

In Irian Jaya, he said, US MAF flew helicopters.

I held on to the wheel. It was lucky no one was coming the other way. My heart was pounding. He went on to say a lot more—about its being a massive country with a stone-age culture, a lot of difficult fixed-wing flying, undiscovered peoples, and so on. But I was driving, and replying, in auto. My mind was solid gone. Helicopters! Two Hughes 500s he had said. Good machines. Ideal for rough country where it was impossible to build airstrips.

And just at the moment they were short of pilots.

This had to be it! Had to be. I left them at the door of the conference centre in a whirl. I really didn't know much about their operation, but surely this must be the opportunity? Got to be. I resolved to tell Mary, but no one else. Together we would see if God would show he was 'in' the idea. If so, then things would, well, work out positively. We hoped.

Nothing happened. The conference wound on inexorably and I, very impatient, despaired of any suitable 'sign'. Finally I decided I must raise the issue myself. On the last day I arrived with the intention of buttonholing the Operations Director, Ernie Addicott, and sounding him out as soon as I could. But he got to me first. I was hailed as I came in the door. Drawing me aside he put his point gently, almost apologetically.

'Er, David. I know you may not have thought about this, or even like the idea, but it's just that I have this feeling that God would have you consider working with US MAF. It would mean flying helicopters,' he added quickly. 'In Irian Jaya. It's in eastern Indonesia, if you don't know already.'

I told him I already did.

My time in US MAF had not been a gentle experience. They insisted, with good reason, on putting me through their own 'candidate' course. They had found over the years there was a lot of glamour associated with the idea, if not the reality, of missionary flying, and that they needed to weed out the Top Gun element before these people got out in 'the field', and killed others. Putting it bluntly. Which was what they generally did.

We—for Mary, Sarah, Nicola and baby Peter had all moved to the USA too—coped with most of the ordinary tests. Not for the first time (and certainly not for the last) were we grateful for the 'P Company' experience. Pressure was something we understood. And much of the course was pressure. Just to see if we would fold. There was also a lot of flying. Unaccountably it was here I met some real problems. Later, with maturity, I have come to realize that spiritual forces work very openly on Christians. And steps 'forward' for the Kingdom of God are often sternly resisted by the spiritual opposition. Personal 'attack' we came to call it. But at the time I was new to the mission business. Plus, of course, there was a certain measure of Top Gun in Marfleet as well . . .

My first mistake was to tell my candidates' assessment Pilot that he was unsafe and dangerous in a helicopter. Yes, OK, I know. But he was. You see, he hadn't done the Sergeant Farmer course, and wasn't the least interested in engine-off landings. Test or no test, I was. Both of us were new to the helicopter we were about to fly off in, and I simply suggested each of us did some auto-rotations before trying anything else. Just to be safe. True, I wasn't the assessment pilot. True, it wasn't my position to comment. True, I was the guest of US MAF at the time . . . oh, well.

Unfortunately he rather made my point for me when on his first attempt we hit the ground so hard we bounced. Nothing dented, except perhaps his pride. But it was a close-run thing. If it had happened for real he'd have been hard pressed to cope. The next one was better. Also unfortunately, mine were fine first time around. Sergeant Farmer shining through. For some reason I was given a bad report. I dunno. No gratitude, some people. I didn't even say, 'I told you so.' Well, not really.

Then there was the business of fixed-wing flying. The point being I still had to do it. If we were going to go to work in Irian Jaya then it was going to be a mixture of helicopter and aeroplane flying for me, and I had to catch up on my weak bits. Fixed-wing. So I got acquainted with the Cessna 185. A sort of tweaked-up flying Transit Van. High-wing, like all Cessna singles, it could carry six people at a push, plus baggage, up to around 400 kilos. Depending on the fuel carried. Full fuel, less weight to uplift, and so on.

For a transport type it flew around the sky quite adventurously, and a powerful engine allied to a tail-wheel configuration gave it some lively characteristics, but in style it possessed all the dramatic glamour of a bowl of cold porridge. A 'tail dragger', in the argot of the air. Tricycle undercarriages (nose wheel instead of tail-wheel) which are all the rage now, were at that time rather too delicate for the rut-jumping, grass-cutting, stone-throwing, mud-slinging landings of general mission flying.

In fact the drama in this type of flying was mostly of my own making. For a start, being used to stopping and floating around over a spot before landing, I found that getting down on to a runway was an almost forgotten feat of airmanship. Landing within ten feet of the threshold was the requirement. I was lucky if I made it half-way down the strip. Perhaps it sounds obtuse but there is a deal of difference between the two types of flying—fixed and rotary—and eye and hand co-ordination are entirely different.

All in all, I was not coming out top of the class. In fact for a lot of the time it looked as though I might soon just be coming out. Except in engineering. That I liked. In the army that sort of thing had all been done for me. But in the jungle I would have to be prepared to do at least some of the essentials myself—and certainly know how to trouble-shoot. I enjoyed all the courses. Cessna and Hughes. I never sat for an engineering licence (something many pilots did), and so stayed effectively dependent on MAF engineers throughout my career, but the technical under-standing I had learned in California certainly stood me in very good stead later as a jungle pilot.

In the end, though, I was accepted by US MAF as a helicopter pilot, and as for the 185, well, they thought that practice, lots of practice, was required. And I did make some improvement. When I was, once again, able to land accurately on a strip I was taken on to learn the 'tricks' of missionary bush flying. At this MAF are the past masters, bar none. Hence high noon at Tombstone Gulch. And now, overflying it, doing my drag act, I hoped, like the desert riders of yesteryear, I was going to finish the day getting out of it in one piece.

One thing I learned in California was that mission flying is a very demanding and highly specialized busi-ness. Except it is not a business. No one could pay you enough to do it. Pilots have even said that to me. The closest commercial operators can get to it are those few who go 'bush flying' in the wastes of northern Canada or the outback of Australia. And even there, albeit someway behind you, there is the back-up of a sophisticated Western culture.

Almost by definition mission aviation takes place in the most remote parts of the Third World, uses mainly single-engined aircraft (because of cost and STOL—Short Take Off and Landing—performance), and flies over very inhospitable country. Though the risks are finely judged, and safety in flight is everything, there is no doubt that this type of work rules out any but the most foolhardy commercial pilot. I know of no one who does it commercially. The Christian convictions I hold with all my heart are the foundation of my flying. They matter more to me than life itself. They have to—to warrant the risks I take, putting these before my family, and myself. But convictions will not replace skill. And to be skilled in this business is not only to learn hard lessons in the art of jungle flying, navigation, weather reading, strip landing and more, but also how to live, work and operate within a stone-age culture. We had to learn to scrap every one of our First World expectations. US MAF at Redlands did their best to give us at least the basics.

Fuel, for instance, would not be offered from some friendly airport fuel bowser or tanker. Most likely it would be in five-gallon 'jerry cans' stacked in the open, and poured—through a mesh-screen filter—into the machine by hand. Our hand. Quality and water content was often highly suspect. And we flew on one engine.

Air traffic control did not exist—effectively—for all or most of the flying we would be doing. In Irian, for example, there was a very simple localized system operated mainly for aircraft flying into Sentani, the airport for the one main town of Jayapura on the north coast. As for the interior, it was entirely up to the missionaries themselves, or the wives of pilots, to listen to the radios, and offer landing and route advice. Often one wife, with a High Frequency radio transceiver turned on in her kitchen, would be monitoring the air operations of a country the size of England, Scotland and Wales! To someone brought up on the norm of European or American controlled airspace with professional ATC, it was unthinkable.

Weather forecasts, of any kind, were unavailable. Any forecasting we did would be ours alone. Based on ground observations at the time of asking, made by missionaries, untrained in any form of meteorological assessment. In Europe and North America—in most places for that matter—you never even move the chocks away without a forecast on board. Here, we would never have one.

Engineering was another thing. There were missionaries who were qualified aircraft engineers—and their standards had to be maintained or the craft didn't fly—but there was no big base back-up. They fixed what they could (which was quite a bit) in the small two-machine hangar on the home base strip. But all power for tools had to come from generators, and all spares and oils and metals had to be flown in. There was no other way. At all.

And there was the flying.

'I want you to imagine,' said one lecturer, 'that the runway outside this classroom is less than half its present length. Say 400 metres. And imagine it is not the smart strip of concrete you see out there right now, but grass, perhaps long grass, with sheep or goats straggling across it. Imagine too that there is a thousand foot drop at one end, and a five hundred foot cliff at the other. You can therefore only approach it by air from one direction. You cannot overshoot or go around again under any circumstances. Once committed you must land.

'Imagine that the surface wind is blowing irregularly at right angles to the line of the strip, and a heavy, low visibility rainstorm has just cleared away, leaving the runway surface pooled, wet and muddy. You are inbound. Of your two passengers one has an open chest wound from an accident or tribal battle. You are taking him to the hospital. He is badly hurt, and has been vomiting blood for the last thirty minutes, which the trained nurse, also from his tribe, has ineffectually swilled further around the cockpit in a panicky attempt to clear it up. She is frightened of flying. You cannot speak more than five words in their language. The plane stinks. Suddenly the aircraft lurches in a downdraft...

'Then,' he continued, a veteran of many years' mission flying, 'you have *a real nice day*. Because for you that's just regular flying!'

But apart from putting the frighteners on us all, they also taught us some interesting, if radical, emergency techniques. One was the 'canyon turn'. Some canyons you can enter and, if you've missed your marks and it's the wrong one through the mountains, you can make a turn and get out again. Most you can't. Then it's either up or . . . in. Often they narrow down like a funnel anyway, and you can't out-climb the cliff at the end. With those you're a dead man the moment you first poke your nose inside. Unless you can do the canyon turn.

First slow right down to eighty knots. Then lower half-flap to give some lift, and tuck hard into the right-hand side of the valley just as close as you dare. Then go for it. You have absolutely nothing to lose. Full power, full flap, over on to port wing tip, and pull a steep wall-of-death turn. Roll out when around, and reduce to half-flap facing the other way. I know it works. I've done it. Interestingly, the early fighter pilots in World War One used a similar technique to jump around quickly on to the tail of an opponent. It was invented by the German ace Max Immellman, and was called the Immellman Turn.

MAF had also fitted the aircraft with one or two special extras to help out when the options got limited. These were items which had been developed over many years' jungle and desert flying, and were now approved and certificated. The most arresting was the Rake Brake. It was the equivalent of throwing out the anchor, and was used if the toe-brakes failed or locked on a slippery runway. A two-pronged rake-like hook was held by a magnetic solenoid up under the tail. If on landing the end of the strip was hoving in sight with no appreciable loss of speed, then you hit the switch and down it dropped, digging in and hopefully bringing you up all standing. There was an immediate mandatory Airworthiness Inspection for the airframe if you ever used it. Mr Cessna hadn't generally planned on anchors being used to stop his planes so the strains imposed on the airframe were rather unorthodox. Still, with a sheer drop at the end of a strip it was good for the pilot to know he had something to fall back on. All the ex-navy pilots thought the world of it.

Another vital addition was the Throttle Return Spring. Not much the pilot had to do with it actually. It was just there. All it did (though the pilots whom it saved wouldn't say 'all') was make sure that if the linkage to the throttle broke or separated for any reason, then the engine went up to full power rather than shutting off. I guess it's pretty obvious why this is nice at 9,000 feet over dense jungle when the throttle lever comes off in your hands. Given a choice which would *you* want? Dead silence, with the accent on dead, or a powerful, if overly noisy, roar from the front end? Quite. No contest really. With full power you can at least choose a strip, and line yourself up for a dead stick landing, with the accent on landing (ie. glide down with no engine—something you regularly practise).

Actually that was another legacy from the First World War. The old rotary-engined fighters—Sopwiths for instance—only had two speeds, full or stop. They landed in much the same way, except they had a little button on the joy-stick to 'blip' or stop the engine briefly, on-off, on-off, whenever they wanted to lose power to come in to land.

Finally, there was the EFS. The Emergency Fuel System. This didn't come from the early days of flying. Though it was so basic it might well have done. It was a simple knob on the panel which, when pulled, poured neat fuel direct from the wing tanks into the induction manifold (air intake)! No carburettor, no injection, nothing. Just in. It could be adjusted, too. Coarsely, but enough to get you home safely if an injector got blocked with dirt or there was water in the fuel line (very possible considering the primitive fuelling arrangements). To my certain knowledge there are three pilots (and their passengers) still this side of heaven thanks to the EFS.

The relevant piece of parched Californian real estate was growing alarmingly slowly in the windscreen. This was not a reflection on the speed with which I was approaching it. A quick check of airspeed showed I was hitting the regulation 80 knots indicated for a good approach. No, it just showed the eventual size of the strip on arrival was never going to be very large. Beside me the Texan grunted and stirred. At least he was a little concerned. Or had he found a rattler in his 501s? I crabbed in towards the leeward end of the outlined landing area like a one-eyed starling checking out the bird table for visitors, all ready to nip on past if stopping looked like causing too much trouble.

I was quite sure that the Cessna wouldn't fit. And I knew if it did it would never leave again. I neared the ground, and pulled the power. Dust swirled out behind me like the sheriff's posse had just rounded the ridge. I bit the dust. I wobbled two wheels along a third of the brief length of the dirt runway before hesitantly lifting the port wing and mainwheel from the ground, cocking the Cessna over on one leg like a coyote finding a cactus. Eccentrically we staggered on twenty feet or so. Thankfully I dropped the airborne wheel back into place, and let the tail lower on to the ground. That was better, now all I had to do was stop.

'A mite soon there, Dave,' he drawled. 'Keep her rollin'.'

I pushed the throttle to the firewall, and lifted first the tail then the nose, and we bored off, up into the bright steel-blue sky, clearing the end of the strip with inches to spare. Run clean outa' town.

Wordless, I went around for another go.

13

Bokondini

I looked up from my air map, and outside to the scenery below, down again at my roughly-written notes, and again through the cockpit windows. Not a clue. Eleven thousand feet over mountain and jungle. My first solo inland to a place called Bokondini. And I was completely lost.

The studious care with which I had made notes when my instructor had pointed out salient ground features the week before had proved totally unavailing. Something that would not have surprised him in the least, seeing the problems I'd had adjusting to flying in Irian Jaya. But this was no problem of flying. This was one of navigation. I really had no excuses. Except perhaps that the whole place was so completely outside my experience that I was little better off finding my way in the air than one of the tribesmen from the villages a mile or so below me. Worse, in fact. Many of them who flew with me later showed an impressively accurate feel for it.

Irian Jaya was simply like nothing I had ever flown over before. What to my old-hand instructor was a featured, informative landscape of curving rivers, distinctive ridges, angled peaks and indented valleys, was to me just an endless vista of jagged mountains and ravines sparingly exposed through a floating feathery cloudscape. It was the clouds in fact which had first got me into trouble. I had been forced to climb hard to get up on top of them but, on letting down again, I was nowhere I should have been. Unexpected drift due to an unknown wind I guessed, though it didn't help me much. Unknowns never do. And the individual features-to-watch-out-for were lost or hidden in the creamy grandeur of high cloud cloaking high country.

I had to admit it was very beautiful. An outspread canvas of undulating, vaporous architecture, with soft furls of cloud flung carelessly around rocketing peaks, or folded in plunging, green-flanked valleys slashed with sparkling waterfalls. Fur stoles thrown around elegant shoulders and tall necks. Bejewelled ladies gowned in green.

It was also terrifying. Somewhere down there I was going to have to land. And it was entirely, I mean entirely, up to me to find out where. There was no radio navigation system, no radar, no local air-traffic controller, nothing. Even my 185's H/F radio was of dubious value. Not knowing where I was meant I couldn't expect the other pilots—who would certainly answer any call I made—to be able to direct me. Given a very accurate description they might have a stab at it, but I wasn't even likely to be good at that. Every feature has a name. And right now I couldn't remember a single one. This bluff, that crag, the other pass, all looked, and sounded, the same to me. They were all just mountains marching on for ever to the far horizon.

It was supposed to be a straightforward flight south-west, from Sentani, the capital's airport on the north coast of Irian, to the strip (class B, if you're wondering) at Bokondini. This was to be our future home, a small MAF base in the interior. Flying time was one hour ten minutes. I had been airborne over two and, although I had identified one or two airstrips en route, right now I couldn't see anywhere to land at all.

The fundamental geography of Irian is simple: it's jungle. Jungle in the lowlands. Jungle in the highlands. Jungle in the swamplands. Jungle wall-to-wall. It is only the density that varies. At least, that is, in the bits people know about. Much of the country is not even on the map. It just appears as a white blank on the air navigation chart. Hundreds of square miles of uncharted forest, mountains, plains and rivers. Perhaps a fifth of the country. A country the size of England, Wales and Scotland combined. Since then I have flown over a lot of the missing bits. They're mostly jungle as well.

Imagine the whole of the UK tipped over and sitting on Wales, with Norfolk at the top. That will give you an idea of the size and shape. It sits just below the Equator, forming one half of a larger island, (the whole being about the size of UK and France combined). This other half, which stretches eastward into the Pacific, is Papua New Guinea or PNG. PNG is quite a separate country. Irian Jaya is Indonesian, though in fact your average Indonesian is racially about as close to the local population of Irian as I am.

The capital, Jayapura, lies forty kilometres from the main airport, which is also the HQ of MAF in the province. Sentani, the 'Heathrow' of Irian, has about the operational pace of a provincial flying club in the UK. It has one runway, and MAF flights are around forty per cent of total movements. Jayapura itself is about the size of a small English seaside town, say Lowestoft, and, if you still have that mental picture of the UK on its side, around about the same place. On the north coast. Now wipe every other city, town and village off the map of the interior, and you've pretty well got the rest sorted. Oh, except perhaps one other: Wamena, village size, in the central highlands. Round about Oxford. Everywhere else the 2.5 million people are living in tiny hamlets. Believe me, there is space to go around. The people live mainly in wooden houses with thatched or tin roofs, often clustered around dirt airstrips. Often not. There are no roads, except short sections on the coast. Probably about a dozen in all. Away from the sea (and rivers) everything moves by air. No, not quite true. Quite a lot moves on foot. On jungle trails. But not very far. On average, one hour on foot equals about a minute in the air. By well-established trails it's a bit quicker. You can see why those who can prefer to fly.

The bulk of the population is made up of tribal groups, with a stone-age culture, mixed with some expatriate Indonesians, normally Javanese, working for the government or the few commercial concerns. Usually mining. Although mission work is extensive, the people are thinly spread in families and singles. The missionaries come, quite literally, from churches all over the world.

Flying due south across the bulk of the country from Sentani you would find the first hundred miles or so—the northern third—mainly flat, and intersected with meandering rivers. All primary rain forest. Flying on, you come upon about eighty miles of high (15,000 feet) mountains forming a band running 400 miles east to west, most of the length of the land. A backbone which stretches across into PNG as well. This is rain forest up to the tree-line, split with rocky streams and dramatic waterfalls which shower down two or three hundred feet into steep gorges.

Flying on south, you leave these central highlands, and enter the southern lowlands—for another hundred-odd miles or so, down to the Arafura Sea, which separates Irian Jaya from Northern Australia. Here you really don't want to go. Hot, flat, humid, malarial, swampy. And that is just the nice part. Living in the mountains was never luxury, but I'd rather have a lifetime there than a day in the southern lowlands.

Just now I was lost in the centre. Looking for our future home base at Bokondini, a single dirt strip some 4,200 feet above sea-level, set in the flat part of a valley. It was the centre for a small government police post of four men, several missionary families and a school. The MAF base consisted of a hangar, workshop and two Cessna 185 aircraft.

I touched the H/F radio switch. Then I let it go. MAF in the field already had some pretty firm opinions as to the value of Marfleet's contribution to the overall operation. I really wasn't about to confirm all their misgivings by occupying the frequency while they attempted to work out where I was. I had the fuel. I would jolly well go on looking until I found something. I turned around, headed back east, and looked down again at the map.

My initial field-training in Irian had not gone well. It was the same old thing. I was a chopper pilot, and my fixed-wing work was just plain scrappy. And one small oversight had added to my burden. In my log-book all my flying hours were mixed up. Helicopter and fixed-wing. So, at a glance, I was a very experienced airman. Judged by this standard, the Cessna 185 orientation course in Sentani had proved me a shocking failure. California had done its best. But it wasn't enough. Not only that, I had just spent six months on the ground in an Indonesian language school, and hadn't been near a plane. Arrival in Irian had been a low time for all of us. Now at last, out on my own, I had been hoping things might improve.

Rigorously I went back over the navigational details. The names rolled awkwardly off the tongue. Bokondini, Lereh, Mumbrano. What I had to find was the Habliflourie Valley. Over that, and I would be almost on to the Bokondini approach. I looked out at the clouds trailing around the mountains, trying to imagine the shapes of the valleys they cloaked. It was hopeless.

Then, as I studied them, I made a discovery. Something that I was to make use of many times again in the future. Instead of trying to separate the rising cloud and the mountains in my mind, trying to imagine the solid ground underneath, I needed only to look at the cloudscape itself. It followed the topography of the landscape below. I looked again, hard. Yes, I could make it out. It fitted the map. My instinct was right, I was way over to the east. I flew on for a few more minutes, and then ducked down underneath the broken overcast cloud through a hole. And there it was! Gateway to Bokondini: the Tagi pass.

You might be wondering why I didn't just fly down through the cloud on instruments. Simple: in Irian, instrument-flying was banned. The clouds were an excellent guide to overall topography, but only that. A guide. If you decided to fly through them you would be as likely to let down into something much more solid—rock. Cumulo-granite clouds we called them. So 'IFR' was strictly forbidden. As was night-flying. Very strictly.

None of the strips had lights or night-landing facilities (they didn't have much in the way of day-time landing facilities either, but at least then the Lord was providing the illumination) so the rule stood: wherever you are, be on the ground by five-thirty. Curfew. On the Equator, sunset is always around six o'clock. And an equatorial sunset is a now-you-see-it-now-you-don't phenomenon, with little or no twilight. After that there's just darkness. Airborne after sunset, and you're history.

Over the pass I thumbed the radio more confidently, checking that Bokondini was clear. It was. Before long it would be Mary I would be asking for that information. Self-consciously I 'dragged' the strip as I shot past overhead, very relieved. Then I ran up to the end of the valley, and turned in to land. 'Bok' is a one-way strip. You come in and go out only from the east.

Flaps down, trim. Check passengers: none. First trips are always just cargo. Ease power, glance at wind-sock for an idea of surface wind, and in gently over the threshold—actually the rim of a sheer drop to a deeper part of the valley. Power off and, stall-warning horn wailing, down on to a three-point landing. I taxied to the hangar, keeping a good look out for stray animals or people, some of whom always came out to meet the plane, in case they approached the whirling propeller. Cut engine on mixture. Mags off. Switches off. Done it. Alone to Bokondini for the first time. Time in the air: two hours, forty minutes. Well, I could only improve.

It was a landing I was to do many hundreds of times, in all weathers and circumstances, over the next eight years. Within weeks Mary and the children had joined me, and we made our home in one of the wooden MAF chalet-style homes which overlooked the runway and hangar. For all its primitive style by Western standards—no regular power, no lights, no pumped water, no phone, no shops, no cars—it was a lovely, lovely place. Mary loved it at first sight. And our bedroom window looked out down the valley into the morning sunrise. It was the sort of view she had always dreamed of having.

I awoke with a start. The insistent tinny ring of the elderly alarm clock penetrating the mists of sleep. It was 0445. Time to start the day. The ringing stopped as the spring unwound. The room, the whole house, was quiet around me. Except. I looked up sharply as there came a scuffle from overhead. Rats. They haunted the place. My best efforts to be rid of them had proved ineffectual. They had been disturbed by the alarm, and had started to race around. A rat race. I know. But that's what it was. They were OK in the roof. It was when they hid in the cutlery drawer, or in the woodpile beside the stove in the kitchen. You learned to watch where you put your hands.

I swung my legs over the side of the bed. You also had to watch where you put your feet. Cockroaches were another problem. What with one thing and another, going to the bathroom in the middle of the night (without lights) was to be avoided. Next to me Mary murmured, and then groaned. She had decided when we arrived in Bokondini that she would get up with me every morning to cook me breakfast. She knew me better than I did myself, because I always seemed to miss lunch, the details of the day crowding in as they did, and I needed a good 'food-start'.

Recently she hadn't been well. She had a strange affliction of the skin, and an unnatural lassitude. Like 'flu. No one seemed to know what it was. But it was beginning to make even getting out of bed a challenge. I lit a candle, fumbling around for the matches on the bedside table. There was no power for lighting until the base generator came on at six. Six in the evening. In any case, there was never any power for cooking. We had a wood-burning stove for everything. Even the simplest cooking operations required the persistence of a footplate fireman from the Flying Scot, combined with the incendiary intuition of a master charcoal-burner. It took us about five years to even get hold of the basics. I flashed it up. The bacon would certainly be well smoked by the time I got around it, I concluded. In a smart move Mary had already placed the kindling inside the oven to make sure it would be bone dry for lighting. Even so it would be half an hour before it was hot. Early morning tea came out of a thermos.

I washed and dressed, and went into the living-room. Lighting another candle I read a Bible passage quietly to myself. Letting the words roll around my mind and lift my soul. I put down the book. The candle flickered and guttered with the movement, casting long shadows, and returning a warm yellow reflection of me and my orange flight-suit from the uncurtained window pane. Outside the night was still black. I closed my eyes. Prayer flooded over me. So little time had I for prayer.

When I took the time, as I tried to do every morning, I discovered so many things to bring to God, and so many things to be thankful for. It was an intimate, quiet and powerful part of the day. The basis for my life. Our work. Without this there would be nothing. Quietly I worship-ped and praised.

There was activity in the kitchen. It included smells and scrapings. I looked up again. The stars looked in on me. That was good. No early morning fog in the valley. A good chance of take off before 05 30. I closed my Bible, Mary on my mind.

'How do you feel?' I entered the kitchen.

'Not good,' she returned, turning carefully away from the stove with my breakfast on a plate. She slumped on to a chair, and watched me eat unenthusiastically.

'Then you shouldn't be up, and should be seeing a doctor,' I commented.

'No, no, I'll be all right. I'm sure I will. It's just all the changes here, I expect. It's just so different. And the extra work. Buying everything raw from the Dani market. Sifting everything, cleaning, boning, carving, hand washing, just . . . everything. Such a lot. And with Jonathan . . .' She stopped, her eyes fixed sightless on the table in a sort of daze. Jonathan was a babe in arms still. And Peter only two. It was a lot to ask. Plus the two girls. But I was sure this wasn't it. I would fly her to the doctor tomorrow. I held her hand across the table, and we prayed together briefly as we always did before we parted for the day. For my safety and her health.

The moment was broken by the sound of a two-stroke motorcycle buzzing past the window, headlight waving and bobbing around in the darkness. Jim Reid, our base manager, on his way to the hangar. My immediate boss, and seriously concerned about time. Using the bike was typical. It was four minutes' walk from his chalet to the hangar. On the bike it was one minute, thirty. So he always used the bike. God hadn't so much given Jim twenty-four hours in the day as 1,440 minutes.

Jim was a man who really loved his pilots. So much so, that he spent most of the precious minutes he saved up during the day talking to them on the radio—wherever he was in the sky. When he left us to return home we all said his departure wasn't so much like losing a pilot as gaining a frequency!

The bike's light illuminated the hangar doors, and died with a cough of the motor. Moments later came a scraping sound as they were opened to reveal the vague outlines of two 185s. A hand torch flashed on and off. Jim was pre-flighting his aircraft. Time for me to go. I put my head around the door to the children's room. Still sleeping. I handed the candle back to Mary, kissed her and, flashing my own torch on and off to avoid the rocks and stones, strode over to the waiting machines. There was a slight relief in the darkness now. Toward the east. Dawn was breaking.

The intense darkness of the valley at night always impressed me. Unlike in a developed country where a 'dark night' means 'dark-with-background-lighting', night in the mountains was just darkness. All around. Like the desert. It sometimes induced a kind of vertigo of the emotions in me, as though I was standing all alone on a forsaken planet, or at the very ends of the earth. How puny did our little glow-worm lights seem, flickering against this background vastness, this deep black.

And then the smells. They were always strong. A cloying mixture of sullen morning dampness, for fog and mist were common, smoky wood fires and rancid pigs' grease, worn by the Dani against the chill of the night.

In the hanger now there was high activity. Beside the aircraft there was Ian McDonough, the other pilot. He had gone from the US Marines to the management of a US airline via bush-flying in Alaska, and then joined MAF. He and I worked well together. We identified. In an operation like MAF you get strong characters with strong ideas but, as in the army, you have to learn to harness those ideas to move forward. Or you end up fighting each other.

Ian helped us all to see that. He especially helped me to concentrate on the purpose, the objective of working in Irian. Building the Kingdom of God, not status for ourselves. Ian once quoted the Bible verses from Paul's letters to Corinth (he lead most of our Bible studies) where the church of Christ is likened to parts of a body, with different people having different gifts. 'Why,' he lamented, 'has God sent all the mouths to Bokondini?!'

Then there was Wenda, the leader of the enthusiastic Dani ground crew. They helped prepare the planes, and load and fuel them under the careful eye of Noldy, our Indonesian foreman. There was a lot of Private Crawley in Wenda. Cheerful, enthusiastic and dedicated, but also capable of working the odd flanker on you if you didn't watch out. The Dani generally loved the aircraft. So much so that they would like to take bits home with them if they could. Tools, pens, parts, all could wander off if you weren't careful. These things weren't stolen. The concept itself was foreign in a culture where many artefacts were shared (livestock was the one thing that certainly wasn't—status depended on it).

But when things from the hangar, or our home for that matter, were 'shared', they disappeared into the myriad huts dotted around the valley—and if they were spanners or special tools for a specific job—then it was frustration all around. The aircraft would have to be grounded. The Dani couldn't understand this. One spanner looked very much like another. And we had so many to choose from!

So with Wenda and his crew we just had to watch things a little more carefully. Mary and I got to know him and his wife Paula and his three children very well. One of our saddest days was when her youngest succumbed to a sudden and rare seizure. He died so quickly we didn't have time to even radio out to the doctor. She came down to our chalet with the little body still cradled in her arms. We just sat on the steps together and cried. The mortality rate among the children was very high, though the mission medical workers had cut it down dramatically.

But basic hygiene was difficult to instil. Invisible spirits they could understand, invisible germs for some reason were more difficult. The Dani had a rule not to name a child until it was over six months old. Just in case it didn't make it.

I greeted them all quickly, and began to pre-flight my own aircraft. This was less of a formality than might be supposed. On a large airbase with trained ground crews everyone spends their time looking for bits that might be wrong with machines on the ground. At Bokondini there was just the pilot. In jungle flying you are out on a limb as it is. So, as with everything else, you are just as thorough as you can possibly be.

As I did the walk around, Wenda and the gang were loading up the cargo bay of the plane—a large 'belly' screwed on to the bottom of the aircraft universally known as the 'pod'. As usual, it was being packed with a wide range of items. Cement, bottles of pills, tinned food, vegetables, computer paper (for word processors), mail of course, and candles. The lot. Over the years I have carried the world in that pod, and yes, eight kitchen sinks.

Ten past five. My plane was loaded, and I helped to push it out in front of the hangar. The first luminous glow of daylight proper was sliding westwards down the valley. Good, still no fog. I was expecting four passengers. There was movement in the hangar. Noldy went in and directed them into the little office. Our departure lounge. It seemed a quaint formality, but we couldn't let people wander in and out of the hangar all the time. Our safety depended upon our equipment being touched by only flight or ground crew. Anyone else—be they tribal Chief, town Governor or local missionary—stayed right outside.

I went into the office to greet them. A Dutch missionary, two Dani medical evangelists—church workers who taught basic hygiene, treated local illnesses, and taught the Bible in the various villages they visited—and an Indonesian government official. The Dutchman was involved in translation work. Most tribes had only spoken language. The Dutchman worked with a tribe, rendering spoken language into writing, using standard linguistic methods, and then set about compiling a vocabulary and, ultimately, a Bible translation. As each tribal grouping in Irian has a different language, and often each village a different dialect, there was a lot of work about for the translator.

Mentally demanding though translation work is, it sometimes brings startling new insights. One translator had got to the biblical command 'give food and drink to your enemies', continuing with, 'for in doing so you will heap red hot coals of fire upon their heads.' He found the impact of his translation on the people so profound that he asked why. 'Oh,' he was told, 'we always torture our captured enemies by putting burning embers in their hair!' They, perhaps more than most, had seen the point of that scripture.

In the office I filled in the flight paperwork. Apart from our own passenger records, there were the forms to be maintained for the Indonesian government and for MAF accounting. I hated the paperwork. There was always too much. In my innocence I had hoped that jungle (as opposed to army) flying might be light on this. If anything it was heavier. At least in the army there was the Squadron Clerk to dump it on. Now there was just me.

In ten minutes we were sitting in the aircraft, and barrelling down the runway. It was light now. Once airborne I trimmed for the climb to the Tagi Pass, at 7,500 feet, one of the three approaches to Bokondini, and called the MAF 'flight-follower' and Sentani Air Traffic—150 miles away. When clearing with Air Traffic they always asked us for fixed courses and flight levels—which is proper procedure. But since both of us knew we were twisting and turning, climbing and descending through the mountains and valleys, this was complete nonsense. But that was how they wanted to play it, so we sent what seemed acceptable information, and left it to them to make up the difference. It was the MAF flight-follower we relied on.

I landed at Danime, and left two of my passengers

there: the official and one evangelist. I picked up two more, and flew on to Wamena. This is the hub of the highlands, and has a decent runway. It was also the base for the helicopters. When I went on to helicopter flying I first had to fly to Wamena in the 185, and take a Hughes on from there. Helicopters are complicated things, and the facilities for maintenance were much better at Wamena.

Wamena was also something of a meeting-place for pilots: Charlie Marvin, an ex-policeman, who was the helicopter instructor; John Miller, another helicopter pilot with a dry sense of humour (he said his last engine-off landing had made him lose his place in his book!); and Gary Willems, a Canadian who flew our Twin Otter turboprop up from Sentani on a regular basis—a sort of feeder run.

Gary was a character, and full of humour. His flying kit was something to behold. Carefree might be one way to describe it. Careless, another. The most dramatic feature were his shoes which smiled at you, having given way at the seams around the front. He said they were comfortable. Later, a rule came out that MAF pilots were to be 'correctly dressed'—which meant that we all had to turn out looking like US airline captains. A little extreme, I thought, though I could see the point. The uniform also looked rather odd with our full flying helmets—which were a wise idea too. Gary got some brand new shoes out of the deal. But he wasn't so pleased. 'You can keep these to bury me in!' he said when he took off his comfortable old smilers for the last time, almost unrecognisable in his white shirt and gold bars.

Much of the (little) spare time we had in Wamena, the pilots spent chewing over flying times past, while chewing over the sandwiches we had prepared for our lunch. Gary always had something remarkable to offer to the conversation. Sometimes we had problems to solve: for example, recovering the fuselage of a crashed Twin Otter.

The Twin Otter had belonged to Merpati, the Indonesian government airline. The pilot had lifted off the runway at Sengi, forty miles from Sentani, just a little too late, and clipped the wing, landing a bit later, mainly in one piece, in the surrounding jungle. MAF decided to perform salvage for all the nice parts it would provide, and bought the aircraft from them for a breaker's price. Small problem: how to extract it from the jungle? Gary had the answer.

'Balloons!' he offered, to the assembled sandwich diners in the back-of-the-hangar club that morning. 'Lots of big met balloons, filled to bursting with helium! The whole thing will be much lighter then. Pull it out with the helicopter, easy. Might not even need that. Might come out all by itself!'

I laughed out loud. The picture of this broken fuselage rising spectre-like out of the rain forest, and being towed back to Sentani behind the Hughes was something out of Jules Verne, and too much to take.

'It might work,' he defended himself. 'Needs thinking through a bit, of course. But has every chance, I'd say,' he concluded.

Collectively we decided, quietly, not to try it. True, we wanted our work to go off with a bang, but not quite like that. But Gary was the best. A heart of gold. And great with the children. He and Kathy had none of their own, so they became sort of fly-in aunt and uncle to ours. Cheerful 'Uncle Gary' was always a popular visitor to Bokondini.

I left the four passengers at Wamena for their flight onward to the coast with Gary in the Otter, picked up more cargo, and flew on to Makki and Tiom, and then back to Wamena with both passengers and cargo, this time bringing some produce back from the remoter valleys. A butchered pig, some sweet potatoes for market, and other crops. Even a trussed goat in a bag, jammed in the pod with the rest of the cargo. Goats were second only to pigs for trading value.

Around lunchtime came a call from Tangma. A woman had badly burned her forearm and side falling into a fire. 'First-and second-degree burns' was the doctor's radio diagnosis. She needed hospital.

Diverting from my cargo run—and radioing my apologies to the the disappointed missionary—I dipped into the Tangma valley, and collected the injured woman. She was in shock, but her sister, who came along with her, proved the worse passenger, moaning loudly at every bump in the sky. I had to keep talking to calm her down. The patient was unconscious by the time I landed. I flew back again to resume the day's work. My schedule of visits, worked out the week before, was supposed to allow for some slack, but not a whole hour and a half out of the day. Lunch went by the board.

The missionary was grumpy on the radio at my missing him out. But cheered considerably on my eventual late landing. Talking, but not helping, I noted, as I fished around in the pod for the right parcels and equipment for him, after he'd read his mail. Postman Pat of the sky, that's me.

I met all kinds. There were the independent types like Thelma Beacroft. She could have had two paratroop Sergeants for breakfast every day, and still been hungry. She didn't need a radio. She could have shouted out the landing instructions from her house, and I'd have heard them. A doctor, she had once been the only female student in (Australian) medical college. She scared the living daylights out of me. But she was universally loved and revered by the tribes in her valley who would probably have worshipped her if she'd let them. To her MAF was responsible for everything. Weather, late arrivals, slip ups in supplies, the lot.

As I trundled to a stop the valley echoed with her ringing tones:

'I've been waiting here, er ... Mr ... er ... for some time!'

'David, Thelma, the name's David. Had a call for a medical case actually . . .'

'Must expect these things, and work around them. It's a long walk up here from my house, you know.'

'Yes, Thelm . . .'

'And *what* is *this*?'

'Milk powder, I . . .'

'I ordered *soap*, David. *Soap* powder is what I ordered. And you bring me *milk*! Can't anyone *read*?'

'Of course, but . . .'

'It's not good enough. I'm trying to help these people, I cannot work if I get brought the wrong things, can I?!'

'No Thelma, but if you would . . .'

When I was feeling brave I would point out that if she only made it clear to us what she wanted we would probably get it right more often. Didn't make any difference. She operated her way, and that was an end to it. The watching Dani loved our discussions. Like Morecombe and Wise to them, I suppose.

'And er . . . Mr . . . er . . . Pilot, er . . . *could* you make sure its tooth powder next time? Thank you *so* much.'

'David, Thelma. The name's *David*!'

I loved her too. A character, but an extraordinarily effective missionary.

There were also the 'Do you have a moment?' requests. Often a friendly face detached from a problem was what was wanted. I saw it as part of my work just to be there to listen, perhaps advise if I could, or pray, if asked. Some missionary work is terribly isolated. Sometimes when I was forced to spend nights away from home, due to the weather clamping down, or a schedule running over, I used to pray that I could really bring some variety, or good cheer, to whoever it was who had to put up with me. I'm sure on many occasions that the one thing they could really have done without was helpful cheery-Brit-MAF dropping by for the evening. But very often it did seem prayers were answered, and that my overnight stays were useful to help someone out in one way or other. I like people, and to be able to give out in that way was a very real reward for me.

I was aware that I could always fly away, whereas most had to stay put—in one valley or with one particular tribe in one village. Quietly working on, unsung. Often alone. Doing good. It was—I mean it—a simple privilege to work for such people. Jesus, though God, washed the feet of his disciples: the most menial task of a slave in first-century Palestine. To recall that service I used to carry a small hand towel with me on the pilot's seat of my aircraft. To remind me I was to be a 'foot-washer' as well. To serve the often quirky, often very human, but very faithful, builders of that real but invisible Kingdom of God.

My second-to-last call of the day was Kobokma. I had five passengers on board—two teachers, and an evangelist with his family. I flew into the valley just as a rainstorm moved on, and was faced with a wet 'C' class strip. But I was happy enough. There was a thirteen per cent uphill slope. That would take the edge off the slippery runway.

I made a normal approach at speed. A bad move. As I touched the brakes the wheels locked, and I began to skid. I hurriedly released them and tried again. There was some effect, but then another skid. I wasn't stopping. I would have to use the rake brake. I blessed the inventor of it as I hit the switch, shouting to the passengers to brace themselves for a sudden jerk. Nothing happened. The prongs had dug in all right, but it was wet mud all the way. The rake had just rolled up a neat ball of the stuff, and the plane went on going. Things began to look less than amazing.

Could I ground-loop and slew the machine sideways across the strip? Not with the brake down. My effective control of the back end was now zero. I reached down quickly to kill the engine and isolate the battery. If we smashed I didn't want any sparks hitting the fuel. The end came soon. Like a drunken ballerina tripping over the final curtain my skidding machine ploughed through a fence, leaped over a ditch, caught on its mainwheels, and tipped over putting its nose in the mud. Its tail lifted, waving gracelessly in the air.

Suddenly everything went quiet. I looked up. Suspended above me were the rather alarmed passengers held by their webbing harnesses and, fortunately, unharmed. Getting them down was a bit like releasing a paratrooper caught up in a tree, but at least they were safe. Shaken and profoundly stirred, I got on the radio. An accident like this, and I would be grounded until further notice pending an investigation. I knew what had gone wrong. Too fast. Inexperience and speed. A combination that has caught out more than one airman over the years.

Oddly there was no damage at all to the aircraft. Not a thing. Stopping the engine had meant the prop wasn't spinning when it touched the grass, which had proved a soft bed, the undercarriage had held over the ditch—I still don't know how—and the rake brake had not pulled on anything solid so the fuselage hadn't been strained. In fact it, and me, were flown out later that day!

I arrived in Bokondini to be greeted by the concerned and unexpected face of Ron Pritz, MAF programme manager for Irian, who had flown in from Sentani. I thought the reception committee was for me. I was wrong. It was for Mary.

'David. Mary is very ill. We think it is a complex of malaria, but we don't know. She must see a doctor right away. Jim will fly you both out.'

I rushed over to our chalet to find two of the pilots' wives in residence. One had taken charge of the children, the other was nursing Mary who was in bed with a high fever. She barely knew I was there. Within minutes we had carried her down the short path into the waiting aircraft, the girls looking on. 'Mummy has to go to the doctor quickly,' was all I had time to say before we were rolling into the sky and heading for hospital. I held her throughout the flight as she wandered in and out of consciousness.

Within minutes of landing, the diagnosis was confirmed. A particularly abnormal and virulent form of the disease had struck. Two days later she went into a coma. I stayed at the hospital. Then another radio message came for me. Little Nicola had been taken ill with convulsions in school back at Bokondini.

What was happening? It was incredible. Here we were, God's gift to MAF in Irian Jaya—and now I was grounded, Mary was in a coma, and little Nicola had been ill again. What did this mean? I was devastated. Later on I understood better. As the years passed we saw many families come out for mission work. Their arrivals were seldom uneventful. Illness, mistakes due to inexperience, problems of living outside a Western culture, all crowded in on them. All this was entirely normal. But it happened with such regularity that it added up, I believe, to something more.

An active faith in Jesus is something that a certain other spiritual being bitterly resents. More than that, something he hates. And an individual, a family, a church, who makes it their business to go out and serve Jesus, as we were trying to do, actively introducing his hope and blessing to others, is inviting his opposition. We were telling stone-age tribesmen they didn't need to murder their children or mutilate their wives to live properly. That spiritual and physical health were best found through Jesus.

And the evil one doesn't like it. For he cannot abide those who bring help and comfort, coming in where he has held sway with fear, death and superstition for so long. So he attacks. Perhaps as an active service soldier, I see battle lines more readily than some. But it's not my theory. In the New Testament, the apostle Paul records his own experiences in part of his letter to Corinth: 'We're not ignorant of Satan's method of operations'; and later writing to Ephesus: 'We're not fighting against flesh and blood, but spiritual powers and organizations.' He knew it too.

It was a very sobering thought that the devil was out to get us, and we were literally fighting for our lives as a consequence. At the time, I at least had the sense to claim in my heart and soul the strong promises of God for Mary and Nicola—and myself. After a few days, with good care, Mary came out of the coma and out of danger, though it was many months before she was well again. With Nicola it was quicker. As with many problems of this sort, though very dramatic, it was all over in a few hours. And it has never recurred.

As for my accident, the flight investigation showed up my lack of experience and I was returned to flying duties, which soon began to include the helicopter.

As the Bible says, after describing how Jesus was tempted in the desert and resisted, 'The devil left him for a while.' But, as he had returned to Jesus, he was to do so to us as well. But for the moment the shadow had passed.

14
Curfew

There was nothing strange about the mother carrying a bulky *noken*, or native string bag, with her. The Dani did it all the time. It was almost their equivalent of a handbag. Except that anyone could carry one, man or women. They used them for everything. From hair-nets to haversacks. Very common, in fact.

My passengers were a Dani missionary family whom I was collecting from Bible college in Karubaga in the west to take on to a village a hundred or so miles away in the south, near Kamur. The father of the family had been appointed by the national church as a minister to a new area. A growing church in need of a pastor. A regular sort of flight. In fact the very essence of my work in the 185.

I packed them all in. Mum, dad, uncle, a dozen chickens, two massive suitcases, cassette recorder, two pigs, three children, books and Bibles, and so on. The normal arrangement was to put the people in the cabin, and the rest, including livestock, secured in whatever way was needed, in the pod. In fact, I thought that was exactly what I had achieved. I glanced back just prior to start-up, and saw mum cuddling the *noken*. Nursing baby, I thought. Securely fastened? Yep. Not much gets out of a *noken*. Then let's go.

Throttle to the firewall, brakes off, and we thundered down the strip, leaving a plume of dust twisting upwards in the whirling air of our wake. Tail up first, build up speed, pull back and up with the nose, and we were airborne, clawing for height to cross the mountain passes.

But all was not well behind me. It sounded as though mother was finding flying a disturbing experience, and was squeaking her protest very loudly in my right ear. There are a number of good reasons for wearing a safety helmet; the main one is in case you hit your head. But it's also great for shutting out intrusive passenger complaints. Things were obviously boiling up behind me. I looked around quickly to see if I could calm her down with a confident it's-going-fine-with-me-in-charge type of smile. The smile froze on my lips. I looked hurriedly back to my instruments. It was I who needed calming down. Clasped to the mother's heaving chest, was an angry snout. Two very determined trotters were scrabbling away at the top of the *noken*. It was a very irritated baby porker!

Seconds later he had achieved what I feared. As he struggled squealing out of the remains of the *noken* he eluded the mother's scrabbling grasp, and bounded forward like an animated heat-seeking missile. He landed on my elevator trim wheel. Swiftly I gave him a very hard pat with my gloved hand, and he shot up on top of the instrument panel. Pausing here only to scream a protest at my cavalier treatment he leaped back through the control yoke, under my left armpit, and into the back seats.

'Get him!' I roared. It was no use. Nobody spoke any English. Mind you, they probably got my drift. But piggy had claimed his freedom, and was doing his best to keep it. Wriggling unscathed through a line of grasping hands, he completed his first circuit, and appeared back in the front, via the right hand seat, vaulting up on top of the instrument panel again. There, my reasonable attempts to remove him in order to see out, only caused him to return sharply to the rear. He repeated the performance. Several times.

Now, anyone observing us from a distance would have

been forgiven for thinking that the aircraft had developed hiccoughs. Every circuit of the cabin that the animal made, meant that I pulled back on the control yoke in my own efforts to grab him or move him off something critical. We were thus performing an interesting series of dips in the sky which did not appear in any flying manual. By this time my flying lacked the serious address and professional finesse that I had been attempting ever since my unfortunate unstoppable landing. This was not help-ing.

I waited until the orbiting piglet had cleared my section of the ship, and was running the gauntlet of hands down the back row, then I leaned over and opened the cockpit window. The roar of the slip-stream drowned out the shrieks from the rear. Next time past this baby was going for a short flight of his own. The noisy realization that the pilot had little sympathy for the plight of their highly mobile asset led to renewed efforts by the handling committee behind me. When it didn't re-appear like Haley's Comet, I concluded that an arrest had been effected.

Twisting around in my seat, I saw the thing being held by uncle in a modified half-nelson, with the *noken* acting as a lasso around its rear trotters. Safe, but not sound. No way was I going to fly down to the south coast with a repeat performance possible at the slip of a *noken*. I radioed Karubaga. I was coming back. Unspecified cargo improperly stowed. On take off, it was secured safely in the pod.

Yes, and I've now heard all the jokes about my plane being a pigsty, and how my flying was getting rasher every day, and when I bring home the bacon, pigs might fly. So you can just forget it.

As with many crises the problem crept up on me unawares. A series of small circumstances building up to an unexpected climax. I had been flying again to Kamur in swamp country, and had finished my work by mid-afternoon. From there the flight back home to Bokondini would take about an hour and fifteen minutes, the last half-hour or so being over the mountains. The time was just after 15 00 hours. Time enough to make it comfortably before the national flying curfew at 17 30. Checking the fuel, I noted that I had a good two-and-a-half hours flying in the tanks. Just to be sure I dipped the tanks manually. Even a bit more, I decided.

I waved the local church leaders goodbye, clambered aboard, and started up. Soon I was climbing out, steady on course, heading north, thankful to be out of the sweaty combination of high humidity and high temperature that was the Southern Lowlands. I had to take my hat off to the workers in the south. They had the toughest of jobs. Particularly when they were tribesmen from the valleys. Like the Dani.

Dani medical and church evangelists ran real risks in the southern plains. They had no natural immunity to the mosquitoes who carried malaria. The mosquitoes in the mountains did not at that time carry such virulent parasites, so malaria up there was virtually unknown. It was one of the delights of Bokondini, not only to be living on the Equator but, because of the 4,000 feet elevation, at the same time to be relieved of so many of the problems equatorial jungle-living can bring.

As the clock ticked round I called Mary who was 'flight-following' for the last two hours of daylight that day. Her clear British accent was a delight to hear as I made my call. And it was the voice from home. None of the 'Say that again' or 'What did you mean David?' that I tended to get from the American, or Australian MAF wives.

I still thought the flight-following operation a little unbelievable. That day the whole of flying in the interior was being run by my wife in the kitchen. For two hours she would be virtually tied to the High Freqency radio and

150

call-up log-book. Every MAF aircraft that moved in the next 120 minutes would make her a minimum of four calls each trip: once before take off, giving location and passenger details; once after take off giving destination and ETA; then on arrival before landing; and finally after landing. A safety check. This covered the vital stages of flight. And, if the trip was over half an hour, or involved tricky routing, she'd get an en route safety call as well.

Her responsibility was to keep track of the calls, and particularly ETAs. Anything overdue by five minutes had to be chased up pronto. In the event, if anyone was overdue it was a matter of only two or three minutes before she came up. It could be her husband. She replied crisply to my information.

'Mike Papa Delta, roger. ETA minute five-seven at Bok, entering South Gap now. Will expect call on top at two-four. David, weather reported building to the south and west over the Tagi pass. Bokondini clear at present. Visibility good.'

'Thanks Mary. Mike Papa Delta, out.'

Weather building. Hmm. It was inevitable really at this time of day. But it was always so unpredictable. My chances still looked good, so far. At worst I was sure I could divert to Wamena and overnight there. Wouldn't be the first time. Weather was the eternal preoccupation of flying in Irian. As we had been warned in California, with no forecasting at all, weather was all as observed. 'Actual' as it is called. What this meant was when it came to reports, there were huge variations in both style and accuracy.

The people on the ground who had radios were the missionaries. Most had strips and were served by the aircraft, and so had learned some elements of weather-craft. But the quality of reporting, like Easter, was a movable feast. They had a stab at it if asked. Local cloud height, precipitation and visibility. That was about all. Of course, the best at it were the pilots' wives. The fact that they were advising their husbands made them feel the responsibility keenly. I know Mary did.

To help her I had taken a series of overlapping photos out of our Bokondini chalet kitchen windows, joined them all up, and pasted the resulting panorama over the sink. On it I named each feature, and each peak and ridge visible from the house. Her forecasting was then based on this.

'Rain and low cloud on the Karubaga pass,' she would radio. 'Dolly Parton and the Wolo covered. Brightest in the west.'

Knowing the valleys well from the air I would then be clear as to the prevailing conditions for a safe approach, without pressing her for heights and figures she wasn't happy to give. Yes, quite right: Dolly Parton was not the official name for one of our most salient features.

But however good Mary was, she couldn't see outside the valley. So I usually had to call up a sequence of people ahead to build up a weather picture of my route. She would also listen to other pilots calling, and tell me if anything seemed to be brewing. At the moment, though there was weather about, it was beatable. I called Wamena. There was a pilot on the ground who gave me a good assessment. I pressed on northward.

The ground began to rise, and I scanned ahead to identify the particular pass into the mountains called the South Gap. It was essential I got the right one. Several years earlier Meno Voth, a Canadian pilot, had been heading north in similar mode, and had mistakenly taken one pass to the right. The entrance looked very similar. It was a fatal decision. Although he had twenty minutes more to fly, the moment he went in he was a dead man. These canyons are all very narrow and look superficially the same when approached from the south. All but one ends in mountains you can't fly over. It was after he died that they started teaching the canyon turn.

I entered the South Gap. All was fine. On time, on

152

course. Then I had to climb. Not only was the pass rising, but the cloud over the interior really had started to mount up. I had to get on top as there was no room underneath over the mountains. But both Mary and Wamena said they still had holes down through. I could make it. As the extra power of the engine in the climb dinned itself into my mind, clawing my way up to 14,000 feet, I began taking my own forecast, spotting the lie of the mountains as usual by the clouds. They all began to look pretty solid to me.

I called Mary again. No, it was still clear with her. But Wamena had bad news. If I could make it in the next ten minutes then I could let down. If not . . . well. I knew I couldn't. I was high on top at around 14,000 feet. It would take me all of that time to get down. Let alone find a hole to get through as well. I crossed Wamena off my mental list of alternatives. But home was clear. Sumo just south of the mountains had been clear when I had passed over as well. At a push, if I had to turn back, I could get in there for the night. It was a small strip, but there was fuel. Cans stacked by the missionaries' hut. I would press on.

'Mike Papa Delta, this is Bokondini, over'.

'Go, Bokondini.'

'David, the Tagi pass looks closed now, and it's started raining the other end of the valley. Cloud is still broken, but filling all the time.'

'Papa Delta, roger. How long have I got, Mary?' I could almost hear her forcing herself to make a decision.

'Ten to fifteen minutes, David.' Her voice was calm and steady.

There wasn't time. I knew it. Not even if she was in error to my benefit by twenty per cent. I couldn't make it. In fact, now I couldn't make it down anywhere in the mountains. I had to return to Sumo at the start of the lowlands. That was clear. I reversed course, and trimmed for level flight. I looked at my watch. Just on five. The climb over cloud had taken a long time. This was going to be rather close. I had half an hour to run to curfew, and a twenty-five minute flight. Still, curfew wasn't darkness. There was half-an-hour's safety margin built in. If I ran over five or even ten minutes it would still be easily light enough to land. Sumo it had to be.

As the plane droned back south over the route I had just so painfully travelled up, I became conscious of something else that the full power climb had dug into. My fuel reserve. By now I had used up over two hours of a two-and-a-half hour endurance. But there was going to be enough. I knew I had underestimated the fuel endurance anyway.

I cleared the mountains and, emerging from the South Gap once again, began to descend. But I couldn't go down far. The clouds had filled in over the southern plains too by now. Thankfully they were not yet solid. I found a hole and got down under. Twenty past five. Ten minutes to curfew. Time to call Sumo.

'Sumo, this is Mike Papa Delta. Can you give me some weather, down there? Over.' The missionary there came back quickly. He had obviously been inside his hut, close to the radio. He soon told me why.

'Yes, Papa Delta. It's raining very hard at the moment. With thunder. It's not good I'm afraid.'

He sounded concerned. He knew the consequences of ignoring the curfew like everyone else. But 'not good' considering my circumstances was still something of an understatement. I was now low enough to sight the strip. Or at least where it should have been. A column of dark vapour blocked the view. Rain falling in sheets from a towering thunderhead right over the strip. No way I could land in that. And I couldn't wait around. I was short of fuel and short of time. It was now on curfew. Not good? Things were real bad.

I changed channels, and called again. This time to Wamena. I needed help fast. The reassuring voice of John Miller came on the line. He was an experienced mission

154

pilot.

'OK, David here's what we do. First: who's flight-following?'

I told him. There was a pregnant pause. He must have been drawing his breath. This he could have done without.

'OK,' he came back. 'Get her to call Sentani. Brief her to stand them by for possible search-and-rescue at first light,' he ordered calmly. 'You'll have to try for Senggo.'

I did as ordered. Mary acknowledged my message briefly, but calmly and firmly. She had done 'P Company' too, remember.

I knew the children would also be listening to the radio in the kitchen now. Sheltering inside our mission chalet out of the rain. In out of the furious storm now moving in driving gusts down the Bokondini valley, and blasting fitfully against the glass of the living-room windows.

John came back on the set.

'David, you must go south till you hit the Eilanden River. Then take a right until you get to the cross of the Senggo river.'

I could see on the map where the two tributaries met. Yes, that should be clear enough. And Senggo was just past both of them again to the south. I looked up as I shaped the course. The sky was already darker from flying beneath storm clouds. But night was racing on as well now. I prayed in a mutter, concentrating on flying a good course and looking for the smooth glint of a river in the roughness of the rain forest below. My hands felt slippery inside the flying gloves I still wore from army days.

'Lord. Live or die. Keep me. Keep me. Be with Mary and the kids.'

'Got the river?' crackled the radio. Yes, I could see a gleam ahead in the fast-gathering gloom.

'Roger. I have it.'

Quarter to six. Less than ten minutes of useful light left. The fuel gauges were jumping off the needles.

155

'Round you go.'

'John, Senggo is to the south of the river 'cross'. Should I try to fly direct?' I quizzed.

'How's the light?' he came back.

'Light's going.'

'Up to you, David. But if you've got to put her down, make it the river. Whatever you do, don't run out of light. You mustn't go down in the rain forest, whatever happens.'

'Roger. Taking the river.'

It would add three minutes to my flight, but, frankly, it was all likely to end before that anyway. I was sorry I didn't know much about ditching. I'd heard I was likely to end up upside down in a high-wing plane. Before sinking. It didn't sound very hopeful.

I droned on into the gathering gloom.

The doctor at the little mission hospital was out for his evening jog at the close of the day. In common with most missionaries in the south he was making use of the last light before a candlelight supper and bed. Essential generator power was reserved for emergencies and operations. Suddenly, he stopped in mid-stride.

In the distance, down on the river, he had heard the sound of an approaching outboard motor. A bit unusual at this time of night. But not impossible. He wondered if he should go down to meet the canoe on the bank side. This late it was probably a casualty, and would need his attention. He would have to go back for his torch. He turned towards the hospital building, and began to jog back. Behind him the sound grew. Suddenly he became aware that it was not on, but *above*, the river. Shocked, he realized it was an aircraft. Looking for a place to land—at this hour!

He increased his speed. They were very likely to need his services soon, and the hospital's. His jaw hardened. Surgeon that he was, he didn't relish the task of picking his way through a smashed plane for the broken bodies of what were almost certainly some of his friends and colleagues. He prayed for the pilot as he ran. In the villages around Senggo, and away to the north as far as Sumo and beyond, others had also heard the lonely droning note of the imperilled machine. It was past curfew. They too knew the implications. Aircraft were part of their lives.

Gongs, drums and urgent shouts quickly called together stone-age congregations in a dozen villages. Tribal church leaders requested bowed heads and silence as they led their Christian people in impromptu prayers. Cooking pots, fires, pigs and roasting poultry were left unattended. They had serious business to bring before God. In the living-rooms and kitchens of missionaries right across the country, one, two, even three hundred miles away, small family groups, people from homelands spread across the globe, had also been called together. In tongues from many different nations, speaking quietly and fervently against the background hiss and crackle of their H/F radios they prayed, listened, and waited.

In Bokondini the on-watch flight-follower put her microphone slowly down on to the open radio log-book in front of her, and took her children in her arms.

'Father, be with Daddy, now,' she said quietly.

Outside her house a band of Dani warriors, each carrying a single large banana leaf for rain protection, stood motionless in the downpour gazing solemnly up at her kitchen window.

The doctor stopped and turned. He could just make out the aircraft as a thin white line in the sky, reflecting the last light of day against a fading background of clouds. The line widened and shortened. The pilot had turned to make his approach. Suddenly, unexpectedly, the noise ceased. Its engine had stopped. In the silence the startled cry of a wild hornbill echoed loudly from the river bank. The plane sank down silently.

157

It was very close now. In the quiet he could hear the air whistling over its wings as it descended. He looked at the end of the strip. Then at the plane. Judging the distance. It might make it. He couldn't tell. It might. He willed it onwards. Once again he broke into a run, back down the way he had come. Towards the runway.

In front of him the plane seemed suddenly to disappear into the ground. Then, in a moment, it had sprung back up again, rolling forward on its main undercarriage down the centre-line of the dirt track runway, its tail dropping quickly down as it lost the last of its flying speed. Safe and well. The deceptive humpbacked curve of the strip had concealed its actual touch down from him. He ran on towards the quickly slowing machine. It came to rest abruptly, stranded awkwardly about two-thirds of the way down the runway, as though exhausted with its final efforts. Its useless propeller windmilling to a stop.

Darkness claimed the land. Breathing hard, the doctor ran up to the plane, ducked under the wing, and wrenched open the cabin door.

Inside the pilot had just finished talking to his wife.

15
Helicopter

The big problem about helicopter flying in Irian was that you were always short of fuel. Not that the Hughes 500 had a particularly bad range. It was just that it used proportionately more fuel per mile than the fixed-wing 185, while landing grounds for refuelling were no more frequent. Almost every operation with the helicopter had to be fuel-planned rather like the old steamer trade routes, which depended on stopping where coal was available.

Normally the Hughes would first be re-located on a placement flight, and then operate out of one base strip, or helipad, in that locale. By 'helipad' of course I mean a clearing in the jungle with fuel drums. This style of operation meant that I would sometimes be away from home for several weeks at a time, but it was the most effective way to use the aircraft. But in terms of work perhaps its best use was visiting those places where little or no contact had been made before, and no strip had been built.

The Hughes was an ideal machine for this work. It had a particularly high undercarriage—skids of course—which meant I could put it down in long grass and other doubtful areas without worrying about fuselage damage. It also had very short rotors which meant not only was there no blade droop on the ground—and everyone getting in could be assured of keeping their heads—but I could tuck in close to cliffs and mountainsides, and land

159

on convenient (I use the word loosely) ledges. That came in handy more than once.

Locating unknown tribes is an adventure. Mainly because you are never sure if you are going to come back.

Unknown tribes? Certainly. Forget what people tell you. There are dozens of them, probably hundreds. When I first started flying in Irian I used to plot the unknown villages I flew over on a map, thinking that the information might be useful for later operations. Mopping up the odd group here and there, as it were. In the end I gave up. There were so many. Though some did have indirect contact with the outside through jungle trading, which was usually how we made our initial approach.

Our main hope was to find someone from a contacted village who could speak the language or dialect of the newly-found village or tribe. As most tribal people speak several languages, it was usually not too much of a problem. But persuading someone to come along sometimes was. And, sometimes, their motives were rather murky. For all you knew your suddenly eager 'interpreter' was in bad favour with the other tribe, and was about to use you (and your impressive machine) as a threat to get even by 'flying' some form of curse in on them. In which case the attempted contact was likely to be cooked up good and proper. And, since we never carried weapons, so were we. Literally. Particularly on our minds in these first encounters was a story about how a group of five missionaries were murdered in the fifties in South America.

They had flown in to make first contact with a tribe called the Aucas, and were killed before they had even moved away from their aircraft. Their deaths sent shock waves around the world Christian community at the time, and the story forms a very significant part of the heritage of MAF. Especially since the tribe were later re-contacted as the result of the efforts of the wives of the murdered missionaries. All of us had read the story—and it had a way of springing to mind just when you were about to hop

160

out of your machine on to unknown territory.

I remember clearly my first new contact. The initiative to make the contact would invariably come from local tribal workers—missionaries, tribal evangelists, even local church leaders. And quite often they would do this on foot. Simply walking from one valley to the next. But sometimes geography or historical tribal boundaries made this impossible. Then I would be called in. On this occasion I took a missionary, tribal evangelist and interpreter.

I had picked them up from a village two valleys away from the one to be approached. The interpreter was a particularly extrovert character with one leg whom I immediately nicknamed Hopalong Cassidy. The offer of two steel axe-heads had, I was told, helped him come to the decision to help us. Though given his condition I wasn't sure how wise he was to accept them.

Anyway, Hopalong now embraced the idea whole-heartedly, and sat in the front of the helicopter pointing this way and that as we skimmed over the rain forest canopy into the new valley. He was one of those who had an instant feel for air navigation. How he did it I don't know, but his finger was like the needle of a radio direction finder. I lifted over the second ridge, and right there was the village we were after. Of course, I said to myself, I could have found it just as well. I hope. After all, we had decided to go there in the first place. The point being, of course, that you cannot afford to get lost in unknown country. Not only will people have a job finding you if you go down. But you can't be sure of the reception either. Anyway an impressive navigator, Hopalong.

We flew slowly over the village, and saw one or two people moving about. They didn't seem over-excited or wildly impressed. Which was a good sign. Too much interest and you got concerned. Almost certainly they had seen machines before, and didn't seem to have attached too much mystical value to their appearing. I pulled on past the huts. A cardinal rule is you never, never land inside a village. Taboos of all kinds exist among spirit-bound peoples, and if you, in ignorance, land in the wrong place then not only are you in great personal danger, but a chance for peaceful contact has been thrown away for perhaps many years.

So I set down carefully on the river bank not far away. River banks are useful places. There is nearly always a flat area to land on, and some space clear of the jungle growth. If anyone wants to start something they have to leave the protection of the foliage, and show themselves. In theory, that gives you time to act. Like get out fast. Trouble was, I had to shut down the engine. It could be a couple of hours before anyone decided to make contact. I couldn't just sit on the bank-side running out of gas. So, shut down it was. The silence seemed fragile after the heartening drumming of the blades, and whine of the transmission. But I kept the radio on. Mary was flight-following.

'Mary, we're on the bank now. I've shut down. There's no movement yet so we're going to open the doors, sit tight and see what happens. I'll call you every five minutes, or if there's movement.'

'Bok, roger. Listening. Out.'

And then we waited. Every five minutes I came up to Mary with nothing to report. After an hour we discussed the possibility of venturing into the jungle, and abandoned it at once. Far too risky.

Then they came. The shore line of the jungle became suddenly darker, no longer green foliage, but black bodies. A large group of warriors, all armed, had stepped out of the jungle. I resisted the temptation to slam the doors, and hit the start button. Instead I prayed quietly that I would stay calm. But calm was not on order. At least not where Hopalong was concerned. Bouncing about like a pogo stick he leaped out of the aircraft, and stormed the line of warriors shouting and waving.

For all we knew, he could have been inciting them to

attack. Fortunately, he wasn't. He hopped up to the leader, and waved first at the sky and then at us. At this the leader nodded. We decided it was time to give Hopalong support and clambered out ourselves, in the extraordinarily courteous, 'No, after you' manner that missionaries sometimes have. I was the most courteous of all. I stayed right by the aircraft.

The warrior leader looked at us all very suspiciously, and then back at Hopalong's leg. There was more discussion. It seemed to centre a good deal on legs, or lack of them. Then the chief gave an order, and the warriors slowly lowered their bows to the ground. I breathed out and took my hand off the starter.

'It looks OK, Mary. I think we're in.'

'Well done. Tell me if you plan to stay for dinner.'

'Ha, ha.'

In fact, I discovered, on this occasion my fears had done the tribe an injustice. These were not cannibals at all. They were very pleased to meet us after all the overflying they'd seen.

The helicopter's ability to go in and out of small and unusual places meant that the helicopter pilots (there were usually three of us in Irian with MAF) were more likely to be involved than others in 'unstructured interface scenarios', as some of our anthropologically-trained colleagues would call it. In plain English, more liable to be shot at.

On one occasion, I was delivering supplies to an airstrip in the making called M'bua. I was flying from an established strip in the mountains called Mapnduma. The resident missionary was away visiting another valley but gave me full instructions on how to find the half-completed landing ground. They were of the 'just past the pub' variety. You know: 'Go east, pass two hills, turn right, and you're there, can't miss it,' and so on. So perhaps I should have expected trouble. But 'ever hopeful, ever sure' as the hymn has it, off I whirled. And very shortly, sure enough, up came the (deserted) landing area. Which, I should mention, like so many of these flat open areas chosen for new airstrips, was a former battle ground. Down I plopped.

Bit quiet, I thought. But looks all right. Just to be sure I checked with the walking missionary on his backpack radio. The details tallied. Runway one-third completed, slope to the side. I started hauling out the supplies, building a small heap by the side of the strip.

About half-way through this operation a feeling crept across me that I was being watched. You know how it is. I straightened up slowly, and turned around. A dark phalanx of heavily-armed and war-painted tribesmen stood purposefully, and silently, at the edge of the strip.

I wondered momentarily if perhaps I had cracked the navigation problem quite as well as I'd thought.

'Much fighting going on near you?' I queried casually on the radio, having slowly clambered back into my machine.

'No-o. Quiet all over,' he came back. 'Now, if you'd said Yiggi—new strip over the next ridge—that'd be different. Always at it there. Not a nice place, Yiggi. Over.'

'Ri-ight.' I said slowly.

Looking through the cockpit perspex I saw the warriors had not moved. But they were all watching. Me.

'Oh, well,' I muttered to myself. 'If you want to know the way—ask a policeman.'

'I'm just going to check something,' I announced on the radio, 'if you wouldn't mind keeping the frequency open for a minute.'

I clambered out once more, and walked carefully over to the passive group. Selecting what I thought was the most helpful face among the assembled ranks, I smiled.

'M'bua?' I queried.

The eyes darkened.

'Ha! Yiggi!' The man stamped his foot.

'M'bua, ya!' The man swept his sharp stabbing spear in a vicious arc inches in front of my face, and stopped it, quivering, in the air pointing across into the next valley.

I held my smile. In addition to attempting to show a cross-cultural mix of dawning realization, apology for disturbing his day, and deep gratitude in my expression all at once. Marcel Marceau would have been impressed. I backed away with a little half-bow, and retreated to the Hughes. The door banged, and I was back in the sky like the SAS on call out.

'I'm sorry to say you might be light one or two items this time around,' I radioed back to the missionary as I sped on across the ridge to M'bua.

Behind me two groups of yelling figures were suddenly leaping and jumping across the small landing space which I had just vacated.

It was working out of Mapnduma one day that I got an insight into the real skill of the people of the forest. Because we controlled the use of so much (air) technology, I know I was sometimes tempted to slip unintentionally into a 'superior Westerner' view. Although we deeply deprecated this attitude in ourselves and others, it was, I think, a very natural response to a stone-age culture. So it was very good now and then to be shown just how impressive the ability and commitment of the tribesmen were when working under pressure.

At the time we were taking a break. Mary and I had flown up to Mapnduma in the 185 with the children for a couple of days. A weekend away would do us all good. Ease the pressure, and so on. But it was not to be.

It was the pandanus nut season. The pandanus nut is a natural crop which grows on tall trees in the mountains. The bearing season draws many of the residents of the valleys up into the heights to harvest the nuts which grow on trees rising from steep and precipitous slopes. It is a risky occupation as it involves climbing high into the trees, and hitting the nuts with long sticks. But it is a highly saleable crop.

We were settling down to a pleasant afternoon tea when the peace was broken by the arrival of a couple of nut-pickers. From their matted and bedraggled state, they had evidently been walking and running a good long way. They soon told the story. One of their number had been seriously injured on the ridge. He had fallen out of a tree, and had certainly broken his leg, possibly worse. They had seen the plane land earlier in the day. So they knew 'the pilot' was about. So they had run down to see if I could help.

I could, but only if they could get him down to Mapnduma, I replied. Then I would be happy to fly him out. They immediately ruled that out. No, that was not possible. He had been injured high up on the mountainside in a place which could only be reached by fit athletic climbers. That was why the nuts were so good up there. It was inaccessible.

What about the helicopter, they asked? Making graphic sounds of beating blades, and a whirling of their arms above their heads. Well, yes of course I could fly to Wamena and collect the helicopter, but, I pointed out, I still had to land somewhere to pick up a man. There was no winching system. And anyway, even if there had been, I couldn't see down through the trees. As things stood the answer was no, I couldn't get to him to help him. Even assuming, I added, that I could find the small group located under the jungle canopy anyway. That was an almost impossible task in itself.

They were distraught. They had been sure that the helicopter was the answer.

I thought about it. How prepared were they to make a considerable effort for this man? Very, they said. OK, I said, you are gong to have to construct a helipad on the side of the mountain.

Give us the details, they replied.

166

So I did. The area to be felled and cleared, above and below the landing site, braces and props to make it level, tough branches to be locked together on top to take the machine's weight, and a clear space to swing out the tail. Privately I thought it was a tall order. I stressed to them that if it wasn't up to spec when I came up then I wouldn't land. I couldn't risk lives. Or the machine. They seemed to understand. They would build it, they assured me, that night.

The other problem I had to solve, assuming they made an acceptable stab at the landing pad, was location. That was a poser. Even assuming I got the right mountain, it was still a tiny green smudge in hundreds of square miles of green foliage. Impossible. It might take forty-eight hours just to complete a simple area search. Then, as I thought about it, a memory stirred. Another helicopter on another mission. But similar problem. A picture of goatherds in the desert came back to me.

'Smoke.' I said. 'You must make smoke. Light a big fire, and then put on as much green wood as it will bear. I will see it from the air.' They nodded enthusiastically and, smiling gratitude and promises, they turned tail and doubled off back into the bush as energetically as if they had done nothing all morning but lie around relaxing. We finished our tea. I wondered honestly how well they would manage.

Next day at first light I flew off to Wamena in the 185, and picked up the Hughes. I had decided to take Mary along in case I needed another pair of hands in the rear cabin on the mountainside. By the time we returned it was mid-morning so I flew straight over to take a look at the area. They'd had about eighteen hours since we'd spoken, and given that they had had to climb back before starting work, they had probably had about twelve hours on the job, mostly in darkness. I wasn't that hopeful.

Very soon we'd spotted a tell-tale twist of smoke in the sky near the top of one of the steepest bluffs. I headed towards it. As I approached I exclaimed out loud. There, suspended in the jungle, on trees jutting out of the mountainside, was the neatest helipad I had ever seen. Open, flat, clear in approach and departure, and correct in every dimension. I came straight in and set down lightly on a meshed carpet of branches supported by half-a-dozen felled trees.

No problem. It was a work of art. Built through the night, without light, and with nothing more sophisticated than an axe. The Royal Engineers could have taken a lesson or two here. It took a matter of seconds only to recover the hurt harvester, whom Mary strapped into the rear seat. I pulled clear to the cheerful shouts and waves of his comrades who, by a supreme effort, had forced the jungle mountainside to surrender their friend.

I flew immediately on to Kenyem where I was met by a 185 who transferred him to hospital. Once there, I heard it was a case of re-setting some very nasty fractures. He had been in a bad fix, but the superb efforts of his friends had saved his legs, and his life. The support and comradeship of a village or tribal community is something from which many of us in the West could learn more.

The first time in Irian I had a critical component failure in mid-flight was with the Hughes. I was down south in swamp country—as I've said, it is a hot part of the world—when all of a sudden the engine oil began to lose its cool. The rather puny rubber band which ran the oil cooler fan off the main rotor transmission had broken, a bit like a fan belt on a car.

There's no cockpit alarm (they fitted one later, as a result), so the first you know about it is when the needle of the temperature gauge starts sweeping round the dial like the airspeed indicator on Concorde. The book says that when this starts to happen you hit the deck immediately, preferably sooner if possible. Only, for me, it wasn't possible. The only thing beneath me was miles and miles of lush jungle, dense as the shag pile in the Hughes Aircraft Company boardroom. But fortunately, in swamp land, there is a lot of water about, and water means rivers and riverbanks. I kept her in the air for a mighty long six minutes while I found one. Fried the engine, but not the machine or myself. Fair enough. Never forget you have a choice.

I then had a delightful three days swamped with sweat and mosquitoes while they took the engine out of the other helicopter in Wamena, and flew it down to me. Ah-ha. You say. Spotted the flaw. Both helicopters now U/S. How did they do it? Sky hooks? No, floatplane.

Down at Boma they had a 185 with floats. In the south many of the communities are river-based, and using a floatplane saves all the trouble of building strips. So, the engine was flown to Boma, and then 'floated' out to me. In the meantime I had stripped the other one down, so it was a humid, but quick, three-hour job to change it over and fly on out. Showed my engineering course at Hughes was worth the time. Of course the proper helicopter engineer flew in with the engine. But at least while he was working I wasn't reduced to 'Head of Spanners and Unhelpful Remarks'.

In fact, I spent quite a lot of time down in the south with the Hughes. Because of river accessibility, much of the area has been 'opened' only as far as decent walking distance from the rivers. All the rest remains relatively out of touch.

In the south, out-of-touch tribes generally mean cannibals. My first brush with them came down here. As usual with the helicopter, it was shortage of fuel that dropped me in it. The strip I was working had run out so I diverted to another, Yanirumah, to fill her up.

As I touched skids a very excited missionary ran up. Breathlessly he told me that my pitching up at that moment was the very best thing since chipped sweet potatoes. A runner had just arrived from a nearby tribe saying the word was out that a village had captured five people, and were about to eat them. Could I go in right away and stop them?

Now this is the sort of request which, while no doubt requiring an instant and spirited response, does give one certain pause for thought.

I wondered just how well we would fare if we dropped in while they were in the middle of pre-dinner drinks all round with every expectation of a good meal, and we went and blew the whistle on the proceedings. Was it not possible that they might see our arrival as the heavenly provision of an extra course? Meals on skids, as it were?

He assured me that, living where he was, he had become something of an expert in tribal gastronomy, and it was all perfectly safe. Anyway, he would come along to do the talking. This sort of business was invariably associated with inter-tribal problems and beliefs, and not directed at us. What we had to do was try to get in there before supper. Our trump card was the threat to call up the Indonesian police if they still decided to go ahead. Murder was still murder, whatever they did with the bodies. Our priority was to get there as fast as possible to stop the killing.

I felt there were still some prevailing weaknesses in the argument, but as things stood, if we could save lives, then I supposed risks would have to be run. I just hadn't quite planned on ending my days as a pot broiler. For a start no one would believe Mary when she came to break the news back home. Still, it had to be said that the Indonesian police were generally feared, through being brought up in the best Chicago tradition of shooting first and asking questions afterwards. So the threat was likely to have some effect.

On another occasion, on Christmas Day actually, there had been some trouble in nearby Wangemallo, to the north-west. Arrows everywhere. The local missionary called the police, and they pitched up shooting as they came. Stopped the war dead in its tracks. On account of the M6 Rifle Carbine having somewhat more stopping power than your regular bow and arrow. But we had only threats. I hoped it would be enough. Whatever, I thought, the atmosphere was likely to be pretty highly charged.

I landed on the edge of the village, and kept everything burning and turning. The missionary got out. He strode sternly and confidently into the compound. I had to hand it to him. He was either very brave or a complete turkey. No, on reflection, that was an unfortunate choice of words.

In a minute or two he re-appeared, indicating that I was to shut down. He pulled open the door.

'Too late!' he mouthed over the roar of the decaying engine.

'They've done it.'

When the engine had stopped I asked him if he was sure. Oh yes, he said, quite sure. He'd asked them about it.

Now that takes some doing. A missionary raising the subject of supper with cannibals. He then explained what turned out to be a very strange business altogether.

It seemed that the tribe had been beset by a run of unknown sickness. This problem had been traced back by the professional tribal spiritist to a group of five unavenged warriors killed in action fifteen years before. They had been lost in a raid, and blood had not been shed in revenge. Now they had come back, and were plaguing the tribe. The short answer was to call out the old enemy, have a battle and kill a few to redress the balance. The chief had thought carefully about this, knowing also very well that his tribe were not the greatest of shakes at fighting. Generally it was they who got killed and wounded, not the opposition. But he accepted the analysis. Something would have to be done. He decided on a radical plan. He would order five of *his own* warriors to be ritually killed and eaten. That would spill the blood required, and hopefully exorcize the problem.

This was what they did. Five were chosen (how was unclear), tied up to stakes in the middle of the river, and shot to death with arrows, their blood being ceremonially washed away by the stream. One apparently escaped under water, badly wounded, to recover later. The others were carved up and distributed at a ritual feast, the only rule being that no one was allowed to eat their own relatives.

All in all, and joking aside, it was a pretty evil and bloody story of spiritual oppression at its very worst.

The missionary, a Dutchman had seen this. A man, a gentle man in every sense, who perhaps surprisingly, despite his work, was not given at all to forcing his Christian views on others. But the Spirit of God took hold of him that night. He laid right into them!

'You say you needed a blood sacrifice to atone for the death of your warriors. Don't you know *anything*? Have I been here for all these years for *nothing*? What do you think Jesus Christ died a bloody death on the cross for? *To atone for death!* And for our sin, which causes it. The payment for sin *is* death. He has offered himself for sacrifice already. There is no need for any more blood to be shed. *No more need!* Do you hear? That is why he did it. That *is* the Gospel.'

Billy Graham couldn't have put it clearer. It was just a bitter shame that four men had had to die to make the point.

16
Meeting

The night was clear, and a bright full moon flooded the valley with light as Moondi made his way cautiously to the meeting place. Quietly he slipped along the jungle trail, his natural woodcraft ensuring that he made little sound. Only the supersensitive animals of the darkness noticed his passing.

Quickly he cleared the village, and began to climb up towards the ridge at the head of the valley. The meeting ground was a fateful choice of location, he reflected as he brushed carefully past the undergrowth which occasionally straggled across the trail. The broken moonbeams by turns illuminated the path ahead, or drenched it in blackness.

He was making for the old high battleground.

The call for the meeting had been passed mysteriously, by word of mouth. His eldest wife had repeated exactly and faithfully what she had been told to tell him by another woman at the washing-stone at the river.

'Moondi, you are summoned to meet in a Council of Elders on the ancient high ground when the full moon has risen above the cleft in the ridge,' came the word.

It was an odd message, and not only from its manner of passing. It spoke of the old days, couched in the terms of the old ways. For there was no formal Council of Elders any more. The structure of tribal organization was now a matter for the central government under the Distant

Chief. True, there was a village Elder and a man set above him, almost like the old Elders of the tribe, and both were Hupla, but these were chosen now as government representatives. 'Village Leader' and 'District Leader' as they were called in the unfamiliar, sharply accented Indonesian tongue.

The government of the Distant Chief was supposed to take note of the views of the Hupla in the leadership choice, but mostly they chose the one they expected to be of best use to them. He didn't have to be liked, just do as the Distant Chief required. And naturally Kwalogo, Moondi's foxy brother, was now District Leader. His ability to be influenced by government requests was second to none.

Moondi had not stood for the post which, under the old regime, would most likely have been his. As the first Village Representative, his brother had made significant government contacts, but to Moondi these did not stand for the real work, or heart, of an Elder. The position of High Elder no longer existed. He had been groomed for *that* position, which his father had held so well. Then, the High Elder was a man of the people. And, once, a warrior. A man who could motivate the tribe to fight well in battles and raids.

Now Moondi could see the deception of the spirits, and the dangers of misplaced faith in ancestors. Now he saw that, glorious though leading a battle was, to do so was to be no more than a tool of the Great Evil, and under his oppression. But, it was glorious! A troop of the best fighting men at your back and an enemy to fight!

He pulled up his thoughts sharply. The work of a High Elder was also a pastoral one. Someone who was wise and caring, who could be approached in confidence and trusted by any in the tribe. Yes, a man of the people. Indeed in the old days the High Elder was often called 'the people'. The tribe was himself. And a good High Elder spent his life involved in everyday matters. Not with

174

government edicts which made no sense most of the time anyway.

So Moondi had refused the suggestion that he oppose his brother for nomination to the appointment. And when his brother had been confirmed as District Leader, he had not offered to lead the village himself. Another had stepped forward for that task.

Instead Moondi had taken an informal post in the steadily growing Christian community at Soba. He had become one of the leadership who organized community activities, and now he concerned himself with the tribe, 'his' people, as part of this. In a way, simply by being himself, he had become an unofficial Elder. People liked and respected him. They listened to him and took his judgments as fair and truthful. They offered him respect.

Yes, in a way he was now a tribal Elder. And this night, with the mysterious traditional phrasing of the message turning around in his mind, this unexpected meeting in darkness had all the ancient mood and temper of a meeting of the old Elders. But as Moondi climbed onward, the expression of his feelings became strange, twisted and tortured, reflected by the flecked, metallic blue-and-white of the moonlit jungle itself. Moondi's bright, Christian spirit rebelled against the primitive shades and spectral wraiths which seemed to be gathering invisibly around. But his heart, bred up to the sound of thudding drums and dancing spears, of incantations for unspeakable offerings, thrilled to recollections of the old ways.

His mind was in conflict, charged with new life; was both sickened and attracted by the reawakening of once-familiar things. Oh, to be a warrior chief! But then: oh, never to have known the love of the Master!

He reached level ground, and came clear of the undergrowth, adopting a lightly poised crouching position, as though ready for attack. Now he stood out clear of the forest undergrowth, he could be seen by anyone ap-

175

proaching. The moonlight slanted coolly across the old battleground.

He waited. Ready. Unmoving. The warrior called to a Council of Elders. And there he remembered. Back to a time now long lost when he had stood at his father's side, heart leaping at the imminent prospect of battle. Here he had killed. A low groan escaped him as the images flashed across his mind. That had been a costly day. He began to shake, and his heart and mind spun into further turmoil.

Then, instantly, unthinking, he leaped in the air, tucked himself round, and squatted down facing the way he had come. His fingers twirled around the short, unsharpened stick, the only weapon he now carried. Even in its confusion, his mind had fired his warrior instincts. The slight noises on the trail behind indicated the approach of another.

A tall, fully armed warrior stepped out of the bushes, and spoke: 'Well met, Moondi, High Elder of the Hupla! I am pleased to see you have not forgotten your true calling. Valley talk spoke otherwise,' drawled the impressive figure.

Moondi did not recognize the stranger. He was not a Hupla warrior, and bore the feathers of a tribal leader.

He replied levelly, 'I am not an ancient Elder, but simply an Elder of the Gathering of Christians in Soba. But name yourself, tall warrior of the dark!'

Moondi still half-crouched in a defensive position, though aware that he was likely to be the loser if attacked.

'I call you Elder. For that is what I know you are. I am Kombala, Elder of the Husage. I am not controlled by Distant Chiefs or fire lances or winged carriers. Foolish things! These men are my bodyguard,' he added. And as he spoke, a group of similarly armed men came forward from the dark edge of the forest margin.

Moondi was astounded. He had been called to a meeting by one of the senior leaders of an associated tribe, who was now treating him as an equal! Not only that, but from this man's dress and manner, it was evidently to be a Council of War. He temporized.

'Welcome to Valley Desa,' said Moondi, 'Elder of the Husage. I am honoured.'

He offered the official tribal greeting, and stood erect, briefly lowering his head courteously as though welcoming an official guest, long expected, on to his home territory.

The man stepped forward and clasped his hand. Again as an equal. 'I have spent two days on the trail to meet you, Moondi. I too am honoured.'

Moondi felt a flood of pride engulf him as the tribal Elder, in full war regalia, bowed his head to him. It had never happened before. Feathers and polished bone glinted in the soft light as the man moved again.

'We must speak in Council,' Kombala continued. When he had signed his bodyguard to withdraw into the forest and stand guard, Kombala and Moondi crouched down and conferred together.

As Moondi had begun to fear, he was not pleased at what Kombala had to say. In brief, Kombala wanted Moondi to join him in a war, to be an ally in a confrontation with the Siep Confederacy, a tribal grouping from a valley to the east. Kombala knew that Siep Spirit Songs had been sung against him because of a dispute over traded wives and, though nothing had happened as yet, he was out to forestall any problems with a large preemptive raid. Kombala knew he would be assured of success with the support and expertise of the Hupla. Particularly that of Moondi, whose reputation was second to none.

Thus confronted, Moondi, as courteously as he could, explained his current position and status in the Hupla to Kombala. He also told him a little about his beliefs, and his present work for the community and the people of the valley. Moondi told Kombala he could not lead his people to war. They were a different people now. Most of them no longer believed that Spirit Songs ruled their lives, even if they had been sung against them. At least, a great many of the people did not, and one of them most certainly was Moondi.

He told the increasingly astonished Husage that he had discovered a greater God than the spirits, one who commanded depths and heights that no spirit ever held, and yet one who had once come to live on earth as a supremely gentle man. Still strong and courageous but one who had healed and given life, not demanded death. Indeed, when misunderstood by his tribe, he had offered himself to die. And was killed by them. His human but godly blood had been shed for all those whose misdeeds demanded death. And, Moondi added, as God, this man had come alive again!

Moondi was caught up with the genuine wonder of his own new experience and, as he talked on to the Husage Elder, the earthy presence of the man's power seemed to fade. As though the Master himself were working away in Moondi's heart as he spoke. Kombala's ancient beliefs were leading him astray, Moondi cautioned. Moondi accepted that he might still take up arms—if one day a very great evil needed opposing—but to go to war over Spirit Songs, or wife trading, something that any Elder worth his feathers might sort out after a brief investigation, that, he now saw, was evil nonsense. Killing for no reason at all.

As he was speaking the Husage Elder began to grunt, shifting his weight from one leg to another. Moondi stopped speaking. He realized he had said too much. He had been carried away by the mix of his natural eloquence and what, he realized, had become very deep convictions.

The Elder stood up slowly, his muscles rippling as he drew himself up to his full height. Moondi stood also, taking a step back. There was sudden menace in the air. The Chief spoke. His voice was filled with a mixture of wonder and contempt.

'You are right, Moondi Jala.' He spat out the name, no longer according it a title. 'You are no Elder. You are not even a warrior. It seems that the Hupla are now content to offer respect to their pig farmers!'

Moondi was abashed at the naked affront in his words.

'I have travelled for two days to speak to a Chief of Warriors. An Elder of the Valleys. One whose reputation has been with me, no, has even inspired me, since boyhood. And I find I meet with a reed.' The Chief laboured the last words slowly, angrily, insultingly. He spat on to the ground, his anger tinged perhaps with the fear that he now had no allies in the fight to which he was committed.

Moondi spoke. He too could scarcely contain his anger. He raised his stick before him as though about to strike. 'Kombala!' he shouted loudly, careless now of interference, though the remoteness of the place made this unlikely. 'You have called me to a meeting. I have come and listened. You will return me that courtesy! Not all that is said at Council is liked by all. That is its purpose. Not to exchange insults. If you dislike new ideas, that is your right. I choose differently. Not all that is new is good, not all is bad. A man, yes even a *warrior*, knows he has to face and judge these changing times as sternly as he faces an enemy. Perhaps with even more courage. For change is unexpected, and its effect unknown; it causes fear and misunderstanding. To be a warrior is to learn to meet and deal with this. I am such a one. I do not choose to fight, not because I cannot, but because I *will* not!'

'Then I remove your choice!' screamed the Husage. He lunged viciously at Moondi with his stabbing spear. Moondi threw his body aside, away from the blow, sacrificing balance for agility. The spear whistled under his arm, and was withdrawn quickly for another strike. But Moondi rolled forward as he fell and, uncoiling beneath the descending arc of the spear, tugged hard at his opponent's legs, toppling him to the ground. Instantly he leaped on to his chest, and held his short stick across the man's windpipe.

Moondi panted out his words, 'If I have come here to War Council, then *you* have just broken the combat law. So it would seem you can accept certain changes, if it suits you. You know it is now my right to kill you for fighting in Council. Now, call off your men,' he concluded fiercely. And he pressed the stick harder against the man's throat, for he could hear the bodyguard, alerted by the shouting, crashing back through the undergrowth.

He eased the pressure.

The man spoke, and the bodyguard halted.

Moondi got up. The Husage Elder did likewise. Both eyed each other warily, though Moondi knew that he was completely at the man's mercy now his supporters had arrived. But the exertion and anger, Moondi's apparently effortless defeat of him, or the fierce but accurate words of his condemnation had drained the warrior leader.

'You are a strange warrior, Moondi,' he murmured, looking down at the ground where he had just lain. 'But you have corrected me aright. You must make your choice, and I, mine.' He paused and looked again directly at Moondi.

'Your beliefs are deep, though they are new, for you have given me my life. To kill an enemy warrior chief would please many ancestors, I think. I acknowledge you as I should. Elder of the Hupla.'

He bowed his head formally and turned abruptly. His bodyguard followed him off into the darkness of the forest trail.

Moondi, shaken from the encounter, stood a long time on the battlefield thinking on the proud man's words. In the heat of anger it had seemed easy to insist on his own choice, but he had been mightily tempted by the offer. To be hailed as an Elder, as a warrior leader, by bands of war-painted warriors, Hupla and Husage. To charge into battle and dance and leap and call. It would have been very fine. But he had said his piece. It had been his choice.

Moondi's first slow steps back down the trail became a run, and the whipping branches and the bushes tore across his legs and chest and face as he plunged down the narrow path to the village. He grunted and groaned as he ran, expressing in his low cries his sense of injustice and disappointment at never having been accorded the honour due to him, never having been given the chance to glory in his skills as an active leader of men. Never having been called Elder by the Hupla.

He stumbled into the clearing by the first huts of the village, and stopped, breathing hard, at the edge of the airstrip, his body bloody from where the brush had caught him. He sank to the ground.

'Jesus, Jesus, Jesus,' he pleaded, whimpering and curling himself down further into the soil. 'I am a warrior. An Elder. What use have you for me? What use am I?'

He lay there until his emotion had eased. Then he slept.

The drone of a winged carrier awoke him. It swept high over the airstrip as it always did before making its approach. And this morning its movement had the desired effect. Startled into wakefulness, Moondi struggled to his feet, and walked slowly clear of the predictable path of its arrival. He sat down on a bank, dozy and still tired after the adventures of the night. In a few moments the carrier appeared, and pretty swirls of dust or spray flared away from its wings as it settled firmly down on the distant end of the strip. Noisily it waddled the length of flattened earth before coughing abruptly to a halt outside the small neat building which was the home and healing centre of the present pale person in Soba.

The healing lady was called Esue. She, of all people, thought Moondi, loved God. She was always pleased to see him or any of the tribe. Indefatigable in her attempts, mostly successful, in healing, and in her devotion to the

181

Hupla, she was a pale person with a transparent love of Jesus and of people.

The carrier controller stepped out and greeted her, plunging almost immediately back into its interior to pull out the items of cargo. Moondi still did not understand fully where the cargo came from, but he did not follow the ridiculous notions of his brother the District Leader (whose ideas had found quite a following higher up the valley) that the artefacts came as a result of personal devotion and reverence to the items themselves. Or perhaps to the carrier. Strangely and wonderfully made though they might be, pots and pans, knives and axes, even salt and spices or woven material, they were not to be worshipped themselves, however beautiful. A cult of cargo was as wrong as it was idiotic. No, they were artefacts. Made by men. One day perhaps they too could make artefacts like that in the valley.

Moondi looked at the carrier. It was a familiar sight to him now—as were the identities of the various controllers—but it still seemed to him a strange and angular imitation of the birds it so much simulated. This ungainly object had brought so much change to the valley. There was, he knew, an even stranger one whose wings whirled around and around above itself. This type never needed a strip. The Distant Chief owned ones like these to carry his fighting men. They were much to be feared, and, Moondi reflected, would almost certainly come buzzing around if tribal fighting started.

Moondi knew this particular controller also sometimes flew a whirling carrier. At Soba they knew him as the 'Balding One', instantly recognizable as he wore a bright, flame-coloured suit that seemed made up of only one single piece of weave. Very cleverly made. Moondi smiled. It was a curious thing that a man should lose his head hair like that. He expected it was a consequence of the great white headdress he wore. Fitting tight around the head, it couldn't help but carry some hair off when removed. Moondi guessed he needed it to help him concentrate on his flying. But he wasn't sure. One day he would know. He had heard (was it from Esue?) that this man had once flown whirling carriers for his own government. His country had a woman as Distant Chief. Most remarkable. The Balding One had controlled whirling carriers for her government. Apparently as a warrior. A sort of 'warrior of the sky' he supposed. He found it difficult to imagine this cheerful, smiling man in the same role as the government police they all so much feared. Perhaps in his land the tribes were gentler with each other. They had after all heard the message of Jesus many years before the Hupla. It stood to reason.

Musing as he watched the Balding One walking around his carrier, Moondi wondered if that man had ever had to give up something he wanted when he had ceased to be a warrior. Was it rank or status in his own community? Certainly working so far away from home must mean he had chosen to forgo community or tribal leadership, if only because here he would be physically unavailable to his own people.

Almost imperceptibly Moondi's inner spirit, squashed and hurt during the confusion and drama of the previous night, began to stir again within him. As he watched, the controller nodded to Esue, and then reached up to touch a part of the carrier. The movement was smooth and deliberate, and the man's stance resembled for a instant that of a spear-thrower in action.

It was a moment only, but a flash of insight, of common recognition, told Moondi that this man, like himself, had indeed once been a fighting warrior. His slim build, his lightly-muscled poise, his quick glance, weighing, evaluating, deciding, told Moondi that this man had truly been trained to battle. In what ways and in what manner he could not even begin to guess. But he was sure of his assessment. If anyone knew what to look for in a trained warrior, he did. And this man was such a man. In a brief instant he knew that here, with him in his valley, was another whose life, now one of service to the Master, had once been one of military service to his own people.

In a surge of personal confidence Moondi was supremely glad that a warrior was flying the carriers in the name of Jesus. The carriers had been the main bearers of the new beginning in the valley. A warrior would understand.

The controller climbed back inside, and in a moment the drumming roar spouted out of the front as the little whirling wing began to spin round, throwing back dust, and buffeting and flattening the grass behind. With intermittent blasts of noise the carrier nudged jerkily forward along the strip. Then, on a continuous wave of sound, it hurtled down the track and lifted up into the sky.

Moondi watched it until it was lost from sight. He felt in his soul there had been something unique in that moment. Perhaps, he thought, he had been granted something of an answer to his prayer.

The two warriors and the noisy, drumming carrier of the sky.

17
Investigator

During my time in the army I had been trained as an aircraft accident inspector. This, of course, is a job which is a profession in itself. A painstaking forensic business which can even lead to the re-construction of a complete plane from its component pieces after an accident. Something that can take years. My course did not qualify me to do that, but it gave me the basics.

In Irian I soon found that even the little I knew made me the best qualified for the job. But it was a bitter business. My first call came while I was taking some time off after the particularly demanding first two years in the country. I was getting the hang of things by now, and had settled into a demanding, but regular, routine. I knew the routes, the people and their needs and how I could help. My flying was improving all the time. And, more important, my weather eye. It was weather that was the killer.

It wasn't notified to me as an emergency. In a sense, it was all over by the time they called me. Our Aero Commander, a twin-engine feeder plane we used between the main interior bases and the coast (the route Gary flew, later on), had called in a routine ETA running up to Sentani. And was heard no more. I was notified grimly by a very shaken Ron Pritz that my services as investigator would be needed when they found the plane. Except that they couldn't. Overflights by 185 and the

Twin Otter in the supposed crash area revealed nothing. As it was dense jungle, this was not surprising. Even so, there should have been something. The rain forest canopy is very high, and something plunging through it doesn't necessarily leave a mark, or only a very small one.

After three days I decided that I should get up to Sentani, and join in the search. I realized that my own presence as investigator would have been valuable from the start, but my experience of this kind of work was slim, and I was learning like all the rest. Already I had a theory: to leave such an invisible crash, it was highly possible that the machine had broken up in mid-air, and so descended vertically in pieces. This was soon confirmed. They found the tail. In dense forest. But this was no help. There was nothing else near by.

For the next two days we combed the area in the Hughes—a depressing, monotonous task. On the morning of the third, I noticed a brown stain in the canopy about half a mile away. About a hundred square feet of the tree-tops had begun to die. I knew what that meant. A fierce fire underneath had killed the undergrowth. Only now was it showing signs on top.

I radioed back. 'I've got it, Ron. About seventeen miles south-west of Sentani. We'll have to go down on the river here, and hike in.'

We put together an expedition, including native trackers, and I flew out to the river bank. We set off. It was a difficult trek. Even if you know where something is in the jungle from above, it is quite different when you try to find it walking through primary, untrailed rain forest. We relied on the trackers almost entirely.

After a stiff four-hour walk we were in the area. We began to search, trying to spy up through the gloom of the under-canopy for burnt or broken foliage. It was the trackers who found it. One stopped and turned to me, after we had hacked through a particularly unpleasant and difficult area of saturated growth.

'I smell death. Over there.' He pointed into another section of dense bush.

'Right.' Tight-lipped, I dared say no more.

We came upon it in a matter of minutes. A smashed and broken half-fuselage, no wings, no tail. Burned, and now wet and putrid. I could smell death, too. It had been there for six days. Nothing moved. I steeled myself. And looked. It was a horrible mess. At first I could see no one, no bodies at all. I started pulling wreckage aside. Then I found them. At least they had all died instantly on impact. Carefully we extracted their remains, and laid them inside the crude boxes we had brought for the purpose.

It was heart-rending. For mental relief I forced my mind back to the business of assessing the cause. Vertical crash. No wings (in fact we never found them) and a tail half-a-mile away. In-flight break-up was obvious. To double check I set about digging out the engines which were buried by the violent force of descent three feet down in the soil. Their damage showed they had been developing power. No failure there. And the wing stubs showed the spars had not failed of their own accord. The wings had literally been ripped off.

We silently made our way back to the helicopter, and flew back to Sentani. The funeral was the next day. The whole business affected me deeply, as it did Ron Pritz, who found it very difficult to forgive himself. As MAF manager he felt accountable though he could bear little, if any, blame. He just felt deeply responsible for his pilots.

As for me, I was borne up by the fellowship of everyone: pilots and missionaries, Mary and the children. MAF suddenly became to me what it purported to be. A fellowship. It was, as I say, a bitter business. But, unlike the experience of losing friends in the army, the caring of the community stayed me from trauma. They helped me carry on.

In my report I concluded that all the evidence pointed

to pilot disorientation in flight, the aircraft developing a steep dive which he tried to correct by pulling back on the the controls to level up. But he was already exceeding the speed limit for that. The wings just broke off under the sudden massive strain. And that was the end. Had he entered cloud? Was it that old killer: weather?

The weather certainly contributed to the second accident that I had to investigate. Though there were other factors. This one affected me less. Perhaps I was hardened to it, or perhaps I was less involved in the immediate clearing up of the crash itself. Indeed that was part of the problem. This time it was a Cessna 206, a single-engine aircraft similar to the 185, outbound from Wamena.

When the news came through, I thought at first it was a simple case of engine failure. Within two hours I arrived on the scene. The crash had been cleared up right enough. The friendly tribesmen had kindly collected every piece of wreckage, and piled them all together in a heap. Now, one of the things an investigator has to do, is to make a detailed study of the location of things as they end up after the crash has happened. 'Move nothing, touch nothing', is the watchword. A bit like Agatha Christie. Now, with the helpful tribesmen, any clues I might have gleaned from the distribution of the wreckage were lost.

At first I tried to get them to put bits back where they had found them. But no one remembered which bit had been theirs, or exactly where they had found it. It was hopeless. So I tried another tack. With the resident missionary (who for obvious reasons wasn't at his most clear) translating, I began to interview eyewitnesses. There was no shortage of these. In fact, so graphic were the accounts of the accident, that piecing them together filled the sky with squadrons of conflicting aircraft all in various stages of departure in desperate circumstances. With black humour I was tempted to write down 'mid-air collision' on the report form. Gradually, though, the truth emerged, as reliable witnesses were separated from the unreliable. Their record of events tallied with the damage on the aircraft.

The pressure had been on for the pilot that morning. His schedule was running behind, and his passengers hadn't helped. The weather was coming down, and he was hurrying to get away. He also had had sharp words with his base manager earlier, and the discussion still rankled. Under pressure, and with a distracted mind, he had taken off and had made too sharp and too steep a turn out of the airfield. He had to avoid both mountains and fast-building cloud. With barely enough take-off airflow over the wings, they couldn't support him at that angle, and the aircraft literally fell out of the sky.

It is so important to remember that people are not machines.

Of course air safety is something that the Indonesian government was keen to improve, and occasionally they pitched in with search-and-rescue troops and support if there was an accident. But as they weren't generally operating in the area, this occasional enthusiasm sometimes came unstuck.

An aircraft flying inland with a full load from one of the other missions (some had their own aircraft, and didn't use our generalized service) was reported missing not far from Bokondini. Air Traffic from Sentani had expected him in on a coast-to-coast flight from the south. He'd gone overdue, and they were worried. Would I go up and take a look? I flew to Wamena, picked up the Hughes, and scoured the area. But there was no sign. I called Sentani who had no further information. I suggested I resume the search at first light, and they said they were alerting the Indonesian Air Force to help.

The next morning I started off again. I decided to try to pin down his route into the mountains by dropping into some of the villages on his planned north-bound route, to see if they remembered him passing over the day before. Sure enough, they did. The tribal people have an amazing memory for times and details. Perhaps it's something to do with not having a written language. In any case, I soon had enough sightings to plot an in-bound track, and very soon had a good idea of the rough area where he had gone missing. I flew across.

At about the same time, a nearby missionary radioed in to say that a couple of Dani had come to him, saying they had heard a plane in trouble. They had been running down the trail for two days in order to break the news, in case it had crashed, and someone was still alive. No, they had not been up the mountain themselves. It was inaccessible. But they knew which one it was.

I flew down, picked one of them up, and he showed me the area, his trail-walking time converting into minutes by air. It wasn't long before I found it. Crashed upright on rocky ground. It was certainly inaccessible—13,700 feet up on the side of a steep mountain. It looked very much as though he had got lost, and had found a granite cloud. The crash site was well to the west of his planned track, though I had begun to suspect as much from the village sighting reports. At nearly 14,000 feet, it was also very, very high.

I flew over without stopping in the thin air. There was no sign of movement. It didn't look very hopeful, but we would have to go in and see. I dropped back down again to lower levels. One of my immediate problems was that at that height I couldn't hover outside ground effect. Very similar to the problems I'd had with the old Sioux in Cyprus. I imagined I could probably run in to land and take off, but that was about all. And I certainly couldn't leave the machine. Still, I would have to try.

I landed back at Wamena, and met the Indonesian Air Force who had turned up mob-handed with their Puma helicopter and a squad of troops. I briefed them, and asked their intentions. Their standard procedure, they told me, was to seal off the crash site, which they intended to do. Great, I said, I'll go up with you and lend a hand. Not so fast, they said. There were one or two problems. Their Puma helicopter wasn't cleared to go above 9,000 feet and, even if it did, how were they to cook up their field rations on the mountainside? At that height water wouldn't boil an egg, let alone their rice. I smiled to myself.

How refreshing to be working with the military mind again!

I pointed out that the Puma regularly crossed 10,000 foot mountains to get in and out of Wamena, with bags of power in hand. I was quite sure, with care, they could make it. Perhaps carrying up just one or two men at a time. With the Hughes I could then lift them the last few hundred feet up on to the ledge. I knew the Puma of old—it was what the RAF used all the time in the UK. But no, they weren't having any of it. Valuable machine. Government property. Must follow the book. Quite right, I was forced to agree. And the rice? Ah, the manual didn't cover that, so they were waiting on a signal from HQ.

I was by now beginning to get their drift. I decided to see what I could do with the Hughes alone. At the base I said that I would be prepared to go up as long as those who came with me were prepared to spend one or more nights on the mountain. If the weather came in or I couldn't maintain the power for any reason they would have to face a wait, possibly for days. Two missionaries and a conservator from the Worldwide Fund for Nature volunteered—and met my requirements. For the first stage I hopped up to a ledge around 7,000 feet, about half-way up to the crash site. There I off-loaded two, plus equipment, and flew on with just the one other.

Up I scrambled into the thinning air, with full pitch and full power, cyclic stirring around like crazy with the lack of bite. As I approached the site, I swept over the lip into ground-effect. Except that there wasn't any. The air was too thin for the ground to make the slightest difference. I let down abruptly on to solid rock. I didn't shut down. I didn't even close the throttle. With power on I could just get off. If I shut down I didn't know if I could ever start up again in this rarefied air. The missionary got out. In a few minutes the man came back, shaking his head. No good, all dead. 'OK,' I said. 'I'll get the others.'

Which is what I did, ferrying them up one at a time and, after that, their tools and equipment. Despite the tense flying I was mighty glad I wasn't going to be the one prising out the bodies. Then the weather came in, and so did the IAF. Fog and cloud. On both counts. The IAF had received clearance to launch their expedition, without rice, and had landed as high up as they dared, disgorging the stick of troops with orders to make for the site on foot. I have mentioned it was inaccessible? They proved it. The fog didn't help much either. They all got lost.

So now there was my crash party plus a six pack of Indonesian squaddies stuck variously up and down the mountainside. And of course with the fog, the IAF called it a day. The squaddies were expendable. Their Puma wasn't.

I had a think. The fog was thick but moving around in well-defined banks, and the cloud looked as though it was skating over the hill rather than hanging around it. I decided to take another look. It was as I had hoped. Flying low I could slide up the mountain quite easily under the cloud. As long as I stayed clear of each bank of fog I would be OK.

A call to the site informed me that the unpleasant work of cutting out bodies was proceeding very slowly so I went off first to look for the troops. One by one I searched them out. It was a bit like the Bible story of the lost sheep, with the shepherd in a helicopter. Anyway, when I found them, the soldiers had got so cold that they were huddling together in pairs under various rocks. They came out when they heard me coming. Fortunately they were all in roughly the same area. So when the ninety-nine plus six had been returned to the fold, I flew back up to the site to recover the body bags and workers.

At that height, as I spun down to the deck, following my fast landing technique I began to discover a problem. I was cold-soaking the airframe: dodging around the fog banks and under sheets of cloud was a soggy business. As I climbed the air temperature outside naturally dropped, and this water began to freeze. And I was icing up. Not much, and it didn't affect the flying ability of the machine, but it did affect my bubble canopy. I couldn't see where I was going.

All was fine while I had the windscreen heater on full. That kept it clear. But that did affect my flying as it diverted power from the engine, and I needed every ounce of lift just to pull clear of the ridge.

I worked out a compromise. As I sat on the mountain while a body bag or tools or whatever was put inside I would keep the windscreen clear with the heater, then for take-off I shut down the heater, pulled the collective through the roof, watched the turbine temperature swing towards the red line, and judder off the ledge. Once clear of the mountain I could dive, ease back the power, and whack on the heater again to keep my view clear down to the lower base. I calculated that while pulling 110 per cent power, I had about four seconds to clear the ledge before the engine went into the red.

Good for Mr Hughes is what I say. Nice machine.

In the end, we cracked it before loss of light, though it was a tough and unpleasant job for the recovery team. The only people who ended the day disgruntled were the IAF. The Puma crew had the sourest expressions on when they left. I asked one of the soldiers what was up.

'Oh, *them*,' he said. 'They're just Air Force. There was a medal in it for them if they'd got us in there. But they didn't.'

He didn't actually say 'stupid bunch of crabs' but then

the Indonesians are much more polite than we are anyway.

As for the cause: I concluded that the pilot had become lost crossing the mountains, perhaps through entering cloud. He had then decided the safest thing to do was turn back south, when in fact he had already, unwittingly, crossed the highest ridge, and was safe and clear to the north. He had run into the mountain in cloud or mist shortly after he had turned. The nose-up angle of impact and full power setting indicated a last desperate attempt to climb clear when he had seen the danger.

The essence of flight safety is continual checks and double checks, thorough experience of operational procedures, aircraft, own limits and local area knowledge. But it is also, as a missionary pilot, what I call a 'spiritual security'. For me, that is people praying for my safety, and myself following biblical guide-lines in my life, and being 'right' with my friends, family and God. Tall order. But I believe God helps. St David? Not at all. Many times I've been down that dark corridor of failure too. There but for the grace of God...

One day I had been having trouble starting the 185. I had had trouble over several days, in fact, and while it didn't actually pose any danger it was annoying. I decided to get it fixed. To be more accurate, I decided to fix it myself. But on the advice of the mechanic at base by radio. It was a simple matter of adjusting the mixture control on the engine. It was the work of minutes on the ground at Wamena to take out the split pin, and rotate the adjustment sleeve the two or three turns recommended.

I checked by radio that I had turned it the right way, and then walked over to the hangar and asked the local mechanic to sight-check what I had done to see it was replaced correctly. He was happy. The only thing I told no one was that I had re-used the split pin. Something you never do. I had a few spare with me but none were the right size. What did it matter? It went back firmly enough, and two engineers had said it was a fine job. I took off. The engine started first kick. Good news all round.

Three days later it was not my day. I had had three consecutive stressful landings. Two 'D' class strips, and one down at Mapnduma again where a storm had blown through, and I had slid the whole length of the strip on landing. I did not end up on my nose. I didn't even need to use the rake brake, but it brought that whole accident back again to me. I was under pressure.

I took off, and headed back east across the highest section of mountains. The weather had begun to build as usual around midday, but it was nothing alarming, and I had survived a messy morning. I felt I should be feeling better. There were no passengers on board. No worrying questions or distracting conversation. But slowly I began to feel as though I was labouring under a most oppressive spiritual weight.

If you've never felt this kind of thing you might find it difficult to imagine, but it is as if your soul or spirit is suddenly trying to swim through treacle, trying to get to the top of the pool for a gulp of air—but it can't. The viscous liquid stops it. Your mind is clear and working fine. You feel fine physically. And yet both body and mind are affected. It is the presence of something wrong, sinister. Oppressive.

I fought it the only way I knew how. I prayed out loud, calling on whatever 'It' was to leave, that 'It' had no hold over me as I was saved by Jesus, and that his death for me had broken any spiritual chains that 'It' was trying to put around me, that his blood spilt on the cross had washed any sin, any wrong that clung to me, any failure of mine, clean away. The devil had no hold. I commanded him in the name of my Lord to go. Now.

To have seen me would have been a mighty odd sight— a sophisticated Western technocrat, with a dozen years or more of exclusive training behind me, thousands of hours in the air, battling with the devil to ensure my flight safety. But I battled, believe me, I battled. That was fight for a para. As they say: I know. I was that soldier.

After a tense period of perhaps ten or fifteen minutes the oppression began to lift. Shortly after I called to land at Mapnduma.

True, I was a bit washed out when I got down, but a cheery chat with the missionary, a fish around in the cargo-pod for her things, and their replacement with some others, and I was back on good form.

I waved her goodbye, and started up. I taxied slowly to the threshold of the airstrip, and paused to check my engine revs. This is a last vital action before committing yourself fully to the powerplant for take-off. There was a healthy surge of power as expected. Then a cough. Then silence. The engine had died on me completely.

Rather shocked, I got out of the cockpit, and walked around to the front cowling and opened up the engine bay. Inside, the mixture control bar had moved into the fully shut-off position. Moving this by a lever from inside the cockpit is the normal way of shutting down the engine after landing. But this had happened without my moving any controls in the cockpit. I looked more closely. The retaining split pin which held the collar in place had disappeared, and the linkage had fallen apart, freeing the bar. The split pin must have just dropped out. The split pin I had failed to renew.

Seconds later—or minutes earlier—and I would have been airborne over a canyon. No EFS, canyon turn or anything else would have saved me. As the missionary walked up with a quizzical expression on her face I shuddered and leant against the aircraft for support. And offered a short prayer of thanks to the Power which had kept it going until I was on the ground.

It is my firm conviction now that the devil is out to kill pilots who fly for Jesus. Nothing less. And if we give him a way in he'll take it. Of course I also believe that death is far from the end. We all do. The devil has no claim on us, dead or alive. But, put coldly: a pilot and plane lost is a material reduction in the efficiency of the mission work in an air-dependent country. And the advance of the gospel of love is something God's enemy wants to put a permanent stop to.

Sometimes, though, there seems no neat, attributable reason for a loss—physical, mental or spiritual. It happens. I was working in the hangar one morning when Mary came running down the path from the chalet. I looked up, suprised and alarmed at her haste. From her expression I knew there was something seriously wrong.

'David, David! Lorraine at Boma. On the radio. The Twin Otter, it's gone down at Ilaga. It's Gary . . .'

We buried him there at Ilaga. In his old shoes as he'd asked. At the funeral we sang the cheerful chorus chosen by him: 'Heaven is a Wonderful Place!' I'm sure he enjoyed it. It's good to know he's there. We all miss him. Uncle Gary.

18
Earthquake

I was on the ground in the 185 when it struck, preparing for take-off. I thought at first that the pig I had just loaded had broken loose in the pod beneath my feet. I was sensitive to such matters. But as I looked outside I could see the Kimyal pigmy tribesmen crouching down, steadying themselves. It was obviously an earth tremor. Possibly a quake, not uncommon in Irian, but usually of minor significance, and with no appreciable effect. Disturbing but not disastrous. The slight movement ceased. I lit up and flew out.

Once airborne I called ahead as usual, and quickly revised my opinion. By the sound of it there were problems in the eastern highlands area. I switched to the standby frequency so I could talk without hogging the flight-watch link. An Irish voice floated out into the helmet speakers. Sue Trenier, the Irish nurse at Soba, was giving a live commentary.

'The house is still shaking but we're all right. No, its shaking more now. I'm going outside. Rocks are coming down the side of the valley, and mud seems to be sliding down. We're all right so far. The house is moving again. Oh!' There was a pause. Then she came back. 'That was a bad one. The house is just shaking and shaking. Shaking itself off its foundations. Please pray. We're OK, though. Have to go and see how people are. I think people are OK. More mud coming down the valley. I've got to get the radio outside . . .'

I decided to chip in when I could.

'Soba, this is Mike Papa Delta. Sue, what about the strip? Look at the strip.'

There was silence as she went out to look.

'David? It's no good. Cracked all across. In three places. But we're all OK so far.'

'OK, Sue, I'll put that out for the others. Papa Delta, out.'

In fact there was little need for me to broadcast it. Pretty nearly everyone was listening in now, and as I flew on west I could hear a number of stations calling in with their own reports, and checking up on those who had mentioned damage. It seemed that the Soba strip was the centre of the quake. Sue had said it was not too bad, but I couldn't believe that a force that would knock her chalet off its foundations had left others unscathed.

The radio crackled again. It was Mike, the other helicopter pilot, who had also been airborne in the Soba area when the first movement had hit.

'Dave, Mike here. I'm back on the ground at Wamena for fuel. Things really didn't look too hot over there.'

'Agreed, Mike. I can't believe that there aren't any casualties. I think we should go in to take a look. The strip is unserviceable. We'll need both the Hughes. I'm diverting to Wamena.'

Most unusually, both helicopters were available at Wamena, and both pilots (one of them myself) flying in the eastern highlands. I hit the metalled runway at Wamena in minutes. Mike's machine was outside the hangar winding up. I taxied in, hit the brakes on the 185, and jumped out.

Mike climbed out of the running Hughes, shouting at me over the urgent whine of the transmission. 'David, you take this one. I'll be with you in the other. Just a pre-flight to do.' He nodded towards Soba. 'Word is, it's getting worse.'

I jumped in, and launched eastwards at the rush.

Moondi walked thoughtfully along the low irregular trail which led along the length of the valley. He sprang smoothly over the small, fast-running streams which erupted out of the valley sides and trickled down to combine and form the small shallow river which wound its way unobtrusively along the valley floor. It was a bright morning and the usual smoky start to the day, with mists left hanging from the fires of the night, had blown away, leaving it clear and warm.

He nodded pastorally to the heads of various households as he walked past their huts. They grunted courteously in reply or raised their hands in familiar greeting. Squatting alone, ruminating, or in groups, discussing the business of the day. In the neat regulated gardens, mothers and children played and worked, hoeing the crops that now not only contributed to their own diet but also supplied an income to live on.

As he neared the end of the village he heard a small commotion. Two women were arguing over the ownership of half a sack of groundnuts. He walked over, and commanded them to be quiet. Then he turned and called to two men who were sitting in a group a little way away. 'Sogona, Honggolek! Come here.' They started up. The Elder was calling.

'A Hupla does not sit while his household is in dispute!' He reprimanded. The two men looked surprised. They had not known they were in dispute. Moondi indicated the two angry women. The men smiled. Ah, the women. They did not worry about the women. They were property, like animals, not really people whose concerns they should share.

'Are they not from your household?' asked Moondi evenly, and a little sternly.

'Yes, but women . . .'

'The Book says you are the head of your household and

particularly responsible for your wives. Their disputes, their lives, are your business. Now resolve their dispute, together!'

The men looked sheepish, and began to question their wives. The views some people held took some believing, they muttered. But he was a respected man, and the son of a High Elder. They applied themselves to the problem.

Moondi walked on, his mind returning to the thoughts of the morning. He was about to start Bible classes. To study The Book. As part of his deepening concern for the village and the importance of the community, Christian or otherwise, he felt an Elder had to know more of the faith which he now stood for, but about which, if he were honest, understood very little.

It had been a difficult decision. He, the son of a High Elder, regarded by many as the rightful leader of the Hupla, and an Elder among the Christians. A man already shouldering spiritual responsibility. He, submit himself to the teaching, to the wisdom, of another? It was almost unheard of. And a Dani at that. But the Dani had been to Bible college. He was educated. And Moondi knew he needed to know more. His pride would have to wait. There were important things at stake. This morning he was to join, with seven others, the class of study held in the Desa valley.

It was just as he reached the level of the airstrip that the ground began to shake. Instinctively he crouched down as did the men and women around him. It would pass. It was quite common. But after a few minutes the ground was still shaking. Possibly more violently, he thought, than at the start. As he looked around a pair of large rocks began to roll downward into the valley to his right. They crashed into the side of a hut, partly stoving in the wooden planks. Moondi didn't like it. Though the ground movement continued he straightened up and, legs spread awkwardly apart to assure better balance, he walked slowly on to the strip.

Suddenly there was another movement which jerked him down on to his knees. A crack appeared in the strip in front of him. He yelled involuntarily. He got back to his feet, and started to run. Then he started to shout.

'Out, out! Get out! Get out of your homes!' This was dangerous. This was a killer. He must get the people out.

Some began to come out at his calling, others to see the effect of the last shudder, others, frightened by the unbelievable feeling of the whole earth moving about under them, stayed where they felt safest: inside.

Then he saw the first landslip. A welter of rocks, earth, trees and mud, dislodged by the cracking, was sliding inexorably down the side of the valley. This time the huts did not stop it. Nothing did. A group of three huts standing by a side-stream seemed simply to disappear, to evaporate, as the debris funnelled down the small water-course. Where the huts had stood was now just an earthy scar. More rocks continued to roll down the hillside.

Moondi shouted again with an urgency bordering on panic. 'Get out! This is your Elder. I say you must get out of your huts now!'

More obeyed him. But the tremors were getting stronger.

'Stay away from the streams!' he screamed.

The people were using the trails to escape. But they ran through the streams. That was the very worst place to go.

There was a scream from behind him as another section of the hillside collapsed. An entire group of huts were knocked to the ground, and Moondi could see through the dust, as the earth bucked and heaved more violently than ever, that they were the homes he had passed through minutes before. They had disappeared into another wall of advancing debris. There, Moondi knew, people had died. He was knocked over again. He started to pray.

He tried once again to force himself to his feet, his mouth chewing on grit and dust. Across the strip he saw

Esue come out of her chalet. She was too far away to shout to, but he saw she had her calling-box in her hand. She was speaking into it. There was another crash, and a rock the size of his head rolled to a halt at his feet. He looked up the way it had come. The whole side of the valley seemed to be marching towards him.

Suddenly an overwhelming fear of the unknown terror all about him gripped him and immobilized him. A fear of unpropitiated spirits and angry ancestors. The wrath of unavenged warriors. Irresistible forces against which he had thrown away all hope of defence. Resignation and acceptance were demanded. A covering of the head in defenceless terror at the end of all things. The vengeance of the gods. A sobbing pleading with his forebears, a resignation to the sentence of death that was being meted out as his only and just desert. It was demanded. He must accept.

Then there came a new voice, one which rose and challenged these desperate feelings. One, he recognized, which had many of the strong qualities of warriorhood he had acquired, and so admired in others. There also came a feeling of anger at the forces arrayed against him. A sense of injustice, of righteous indignation. Of a need to work and strive to oppose this terrible disaster overtaking his valley and his people. He wanted to succumb to his initial fears. But his spirit told him that the latter was right.

But the ancient fear was too strong. He sank down on to the tortured ground. He was not able to fight any more. He would accept his fate.

'Oh, God,' he whispered, through smeared and broken lips, 'help my people. I cannot.'

Then, in the distance, faintly, over the hideous splintering and thudding of collapsing dwellings, the roar and rumble of down-rushing mud and rocks, the crackling of fires ignited by blazing cooking embers, there came a noise like the irritating buzz of an insect, a noise which grew slowly but surely into the regular high-pitched drumming that he knew so well. It was a carrier! One of the carriers was coming!

He raised his head. The carrier, one of the whirling type, was roaring down the valley fast and low, the noise building and thrumming, urgent and decisive, irresistibly single-minded and triumphant over the mindless chaos on the ground. It raced toward him only a few feet above the ground, the clatter of it rose to a sense-shattering pitch.

Moondi stayed still, letting the beating sound soak through him, and pummel at his mind and body, filling his senses as it swept over, exalting and thrilling in the speed and noisy spirit of the carrier. He caught sight of a white domed head and bright orange clothing as it stormed past.

And his heart changed. He knew now that it was for this that he had been prepared. This was the moment of his calling. Moondi turned over, set his face the way he had done beside his father on that ancient, high field so many years before, and went forward in to battle.

Scrabbling, half on his hands, half standing, he got up and began to run.

'Come on!' he bellowed as loudly as his mud-filled mouth would permit. 'My Hupla, this way!'

One or two who had been crouching nearby saw his movement, and began to follow him. Moondi would know, they said. One or two more got up, as did others who had been too frightened to move. Moondi looked around, his mind judging, assessing, deciding. Where would be safest? Back down on the strip or higher up the valley sides? He glanced around quickly trying to peer through the smoke and dust. Those down on the strip were best off there. The slips couldn't reach them there. But up the valley side the only answer was to climb.

Quickly he cautioned those with him to stay down on the strip, and congregate near Esue's chalet. There some of them could perhaps help with the wounded. He and another Christian Elder would climb up higher, and take those on the valley side up to the ridge, avoiding the streams. He set off with his companion, half-striding, half-running, half-dancing in this crazy moving world.

'Up here!' He continued to shout and exhort as the straggling group he had collected followed him up the mountainside. He was high up in the lead, and he watched the hillside above like a warrior watching for arrows and spears. He was watching for rocks and stones. One blow from above could kill outright. Indeed, already had. But, as the stones came down, he spotted them, and shouted a warning to those following, holding up a broken piece of board from a hut, as some protection. Their eyes were their best defence in dodging the deadly showers. After a desperate climb they were at last up high enough to be out of danger. As long as they stayed on exposed solid rock near the ridge they would be all right.

Moondi looked across the valley. Others too had followed his example. No longer were groups sitting huddled together, waiting for their fate. They were scrabbling, climbing, hauling themselves up to safety. Moondi recognized some of them. And some of those in the lead. They were the Elders. There they were, each of them, leading the people to safety!

Another whirling carrier lifted up over the ridge, and sank down towards the airstrip. Another to help. That was good. At least the injured had a chance. He looked around and, seeing the group secure, launched himself back down again into the smoky confusion. There would be others he could help. He must. It was his duty.

As I swung over the valley I was aghast at the damage. The half-dozen or so peaceful settlements that represented the Hupla tribe in the valley were smashed and riven beyond any semblance of their former shape. Four of the villages were almost completely destroyed; only here and there were isolated groups of huts still standing. Two others, including Soba itself, were in mildly better shape with over half the dwellings still intact. But all the time fresh tremors shook the region and, with each, a fall of rock or, worse, a slide of land would destroy something further.

The neat picturesque gardens of which the Hupla were so proud, latticed together like an old-time set of English allotments, regular and organized, had been swept away. They had been prime targets for the mudslides, situated high up on the now-heaving flanks of the valley. And, I realized with a shock, so had been the people: the women and children who would normally be working in them, tilling and hoeing, this time of the morning.

I flew down the length of the valley, and out again, reporting the scene on the radio, formally stating that a major disaster had occurred, and that the authorities needed to be prepared for massive disaster relief. I carried straight on and landed in Holuwon. I was going to need help with this. An air crewman. John Wilson, the Yali-translating Scot would be a firm hand in a crisis, and he could speak the Yali language understood by the Hupla.

By comparison his valley seemed almost untouched, and it was only six minutes' flight away. He climbed in, and I talked more on the radio and some to him.

'I think the best thing is to get people out and higher up if possible. Or down on to the strip. It's no use for the 185s, and far enough away from the valley sides to be safe. As long as it doesn't crack any more,' I added.

'I think we're going to have to let the fit ones take care of themselves first, David. You've got to get the injured out.'

He was right. I couldn't start lifting thousands of people around the valley. Not with dead and dying in urgent need.

'Injured first, it is,' I agreed. 'We'll lift them on to the strip.'

I called Wamena to see if they knew if Passema was open. It wasn't far away, and they could get a 185 in there if it was clear. We were going to need fixed-wing support—for hospital cases, for a start. And for fuel. There was nothing at Soba.

Mike Meeuwse was airborne in the other Hughes, and had begun his own sweep down the valley. He was as shocked as I. Though he must have already had some impression from his first overflight.

'It's just all gone,' he radioed in disbelief. 'Just smashed to pieces.'

We hurriedly agreed a co-ordinated rescue programme. Taking one side of the valley each, lifting the injured down on to the strip where Sue, assuming she was up to it, would give first aid, and triage the hospital cases. These we would fly out to Passema (which I now knew was open) for our fixed-winged aircraft to carry them to hospital, and return with fuel.

Working slowly from village to village, and concentrating in the area of the mudslips and rock falls, we began to get the injured people out. Some just climbed in, and were ferried down on to the strip in a matter of seconds. Others took longer, and had to be helped into the machine by John and other nearby Hupla. Broken arms, legs, and cuts and bruises, there were a few. But in the main the injuries were caused by suffocation or crushing.

I gave up counting trips as I reached fifty take offs and landings. The official limit for one day's operation was supposed to be twenty.

All day the shocks continued, rocks and mudslips rushing down like melting snow off a roof, smothering whatever was below. On one sortie I saw three of the remaining huts suddenly swept down by a vicious torrent of mud, and burst dramatically into flames as the thatched roofs touched the cooking fires. Smoke from this and other fires had streamed down into the valley, and added a warlike feel to the rescue operation. Now there was a serious danger of collision. The two Hughes were dodging about the valley like summer dragonflies. It meant continuous radio work to make sure we each knew where the other was.

The visibility was dreadful. The operation became relentless: call Mike with position, lift off and dip down through dust and smoke, hover and look about. Spot a casualty. Land as near as possible. Call Mike for landing. Pick 'em up, bundle them in to the cabin. Call Mike for take off, and transit to strip. Down. Bundle out. Check with Sue for triaged cases to Passema. Divert, or return back up the valley. Fuelling, rotors running, at Passema when needed.

The strain was beginning to tell on both of us. Though I had the pressure of flying, John had the continual task of leaping out and helping or lifting frightened and protesting, and often seriously hurt, victims into the helicopter. In some places I could leave the machine running (the blessed Hughes is fortunate in that way), and get out to help him. But most of the time I wanted to be in that seat ready to pull away if the land started to slip from under us. With shocks still striking, every moment I spent out of the cockpit exposed fifty per cent of our air rescue 'assets' not to mention ourselves, to sudden damage.

Having cleared most of the walkers and visible victims, I began to make wide circular searches, hovering over previously visited slips to see if we could spot, and get out, some of those buried there. This proved precarious in two ways. First, because of the need to fly close to the valley sides, and land actually on the slips. Second, John had to get out and walk around on very unstable earth, which could slip or move at any moment. It was also very grim.

Many of the people, we could see, were beyond the help of our hands. Of those, we got out the ones we could, but other bodies had to wait many days before being recovered for Hupla cremation. Still others were effectively sealed in their own graves. I would dip low over a patch of bare ground surrounded by slips or broken-down trees, and a head would move, or a hand or foot wave, and down we would go.

The helicopter was now caked with mud and blood. The noise was continual, and the smoke clouds made us cough. Focussing on the instruments for power and limit checks before lifting became too familiar a chore, making it more difficult, and progressively the locations where we found people trapped were demanding more and more from my flying when I had less and less to give. Around mid-afternoon we agreed to take a break. We flew down to the strip, got out, and then crouched groggily for a moment by the filthy machines. Sue came to join us.

'Please pray for this to stop!' she pleaded, exhausted from the shattering emotion of seeing her valley and home destroyed, the people she loved and cared for killed and injured all around her, and reeling from the continual demand on her medical skills. We told her we had been. All morning. As we were flying.

I drank a pint of water, and crammed the sandwiches Mary had made for my 185 trip early that morning into my mouth. I pulled the sweat-cooled helmet back over my head and forced myself to my feet. If ever I needed para stamina allied to flying skill it was now.

'I'm getting back up there.' Mike got up too.

The afternoon continued. The flights were longer and less rewarding. Only occasionally now did we find casualties. Though there was one very bad moment when a group who had thought themselves high enough up to be safe found they were on top of the beginning of a slip.

At one point I spotted three men on a ledge. Two were injured. They were inaccessible. The slope was too steep for me to set down. And hovering would bring the rotors into contact with the valley sides. What to do? I noticed a rock.

'John, if I put a skid on that, could you get out and help

them?'

He nodded so I inched in, glancing from rock to rotor tip and back again. I felt the skid touch. I held the machine steady. Rotor blades two feet from the valley side. John then opened his right hand door slowly, and climbed down on to the airborne skid, hanging on for dear life in the blast of the downwash. He then climbed under the cabin to the other skid, and on to the dubious security of the rock. He waved, and I pulled clear.

I hovered nearby as he walked uphill, and spoke to the Hupla. He indicated to them what they had to do. They did not like it, supposing the machine capable of landing. He waved again. This was their only option. They half-crawled and half-walked painfully down to the rock. I flew back in, covering them with my blades. John yanked open the rear door and, standing there, helped them one at a time up on to the rock, and then up inside the rear cabin. I gently fed in power to keep us steady as the machine weighed down heavily with the injured.

Two inside, and I shouted him clear. Up through the rotors I could see stones rolling down on to us. I pushed the cyclic and we jerked clear of the rock just as a dozen cricket balls bounded past. John and the remaining Hupla crouched in the lee of the rock. 'One of those in my rotors,' I thought, 'and goodnight sweet prince.'

I moved back in. Skid on the rock, steady, and John climbed up and pulled the rear door back open. He heaved the third man in and, closing the now full rear section, clambered back underneath the helicopter on to the flying outboard skid, reached up, opened his door, and hoisted himself back inside. I pulled clear and made for the strip.

Moondi leaned wearily against one of the few trees which remained standing in that part of the valley. He had been working all day to collect frightened, often hysterical, Hupla into groups, and climb them up or down the treacherous slopes to safety. It had been a day wearing on the nerves, emotions and, above all, on the body. He was dead beat. Everyone else was pretty much the same. And the sun, red, through the smoke and haze of the disaster, was now low in the sky. He just wanted to sink down where he stood, and sleep.

Then he saw something that made his blood run cold. On the opposite side of the bluff in which he was standing a small group, three women and a child, seemed to have stumbled into a slow mudslip. They were trying to pull themselves up but they were being carried steadily downwards all the while. One would struggle round and seem to get to her feet, pick up the child, and then almost at once topple back into the slowly moving mass again. The others tried to help, but they too fell back to suffer the same fate.

Immediately Moondi forgot his exhaustion, and set off down the hillside to climb the other. This was the dangerous side. As he did so he felt the earth buck once again beneath him as another movement hit the valley. The earth he stood on began to move. Quickly, he sprang sideways across to surer ground. He was close to the women now.

As he reached them, they began screaming in terror, and floundering about more desperately, for the surge had begun to slip away faster under the impulse of the latest tremor. He made a quick decision. In two leaps he was with them. As he sank into the moving mud he grabbed the arm of one of them, and heaved her up powerfully out of the mire, forcing her on to a small strip of firm ground which seemed to separate the moving flow, no more than an arm's length away. She fell half on to it, and managed to pull herself out with a root, crawling round and holding her hands out, screaming for the child. Moondi threw it to her. It landed bawling in the mud by her side.

Then he pushed first one woman, and then the other, as hard as he could up on to the surface of the slippery mobile landslide and towards the grasping arms of the woman who had reached firmer ground. One by one she pulled them across herself to the comparative safety of the static tongue of land.

This effort had pushed Moondi further down into the now fast-moving slip and, fight it as he could, he sank further and further into the tumbling cataract of earth and rock. Vaguely he heard the sound of the women's voices screaming, then these fell silent. He began to cough and choke on the mud which now filled his mouth and throat. His struggles grew weaker and weaker. Soon he struggled no more.

He felt he could hear a voice, the voice of someone he knew, or had known once, very well. Lanya? Was it her? The voice of his first wife. His own beloved? It bore all the richness, all the warmly remembered flavour. But no, it was stronger, more manly. Altogether greater. In fact it seemed to be the voice of Someone very much greater.

The rocks pounded against his back, and the earth smothered his face. The women were screaming again. But Moondi could no longer hear them.

We deposited the injured, and took off again. I made a long sweep back along the valley side spotting a small group caught between two slips on a sort of island of mud. They were lying very still, and had probably been buried. A further slip had re-exposed them. Or perhaps they had just managed to pull themselves clear before collapsing exhausted. It looked like two, possibly three, women and a child. I came down low over the supine bodies, the soft mud rippling and moving away from the downwash. There didn't seem to be any movement. Nothing at all. I swung the machine around. John looked down from his side.

'No.' He could see no hope either.

I lifted the collective, and the sound of the blades clattered harshly back from the valley sides as we moved slowly away to look elsewhere. It was sight we had seen too much of that day. Then I turned around. I don't know why. I just felt perhaps a still small voice saying, 'Look again.' I floated back over the same ground. Suddenly John tensed.

'The child's hand. It moved. I'm sure it moved!'

'Right.' I dipped down lower, and put the skids on the rough ledge. John jumped out and caught hold of the child, carrying it back to the helicopter in his arms, and laying it on the seat. It was alive, barely. So were the others. But the location meant that I couldn't get out. And he couldn't drag them across alone. I had to get more help. Leaving him there, I lifted off and returned to the strip. Two Hupla bundled in. In minutes I was back again and strong arms were lifting the barely breathing survivors into the back.

I eased away off the hillside.

Mike and I worked until nearly dark, flying well over a hundred sorties between us. We flew back to Wamena, and slept there. We couldn't risk leaving the machines on the ground at Soba overnight. The shocks were lessening all the time, but still very evident. We could feel them distinctly at Wamena. It wasn't a restful night, exhausted though we were. We prayed and slept, slept and prayed. The rock falls and slides we knew were still happening. None of us felt much restored when we woke at the dawn to fly out to see a new scene of devastation.

For the next three or four days we continued searching. By day four I had had enough. I was at the limit. Pre-dawn, readying the helicopter. In my mind more sick, injured and devastated people faced me, rising up before me like the mists before an Irian sunrise. I leant against the machine. It was wet with dew.

'Oh, Father God!' I said. 'I need more strength.' Unbidden, the words of Isaiah slipped into my mind: 'They that wait upon the Lord shall renew their strength...'

I climbed into the aircraft, and pressed the starter. The

machine rose up steadily into the valley dawn, the beating blades echoing back off the steep crags and outcrops as I flew.

I had been given my wings.

As the days turned into weeks, the tremors gradually ceased, and the countryside stopped threatening to move. The government began to organize blankets, rice and other supplies. But we saw nothing of the big Air Force Pumas that would have been so helpful in moving people and supplies around.

Over the following months MAF and the Hupla repaired the strip, and managed to evacuate most of the people into safer parts of the valley. We also had to bring in all their food. It was a massive logistics exercise. But, with the strip restored, the Cessnas managed to keep the valley folk alive.

When we left Irian to return to England in the summer of 1990, MAF was still hauling in tons of food to support the survivors, and Sue Trenier had rebuilt part of her mission chalet and clinic at Soba. Some of the village dwellings had been restored as had some of the gardens for vital produce. It had been devastated but the signs of rebirth were already there.

A few weeks before we left, Mary and I and the boys flew into Soba for a Christian service to say a 'goodbye'. For us it was profoundly moving. As we sang the songs along with the tribesmen and women, I realized that, until the earthquake, they had been just one tribe out of the peoples we had served in our time in Irian Jaya. We looked around now at the faces, many of whom, I knew, we had pulled out of the grasping mud on that fateful day. They were now restored and healthy. Ready and willing to rebuild what had been lost. Mary pointed out a group of three women and a child. They caught our eyes, and smiled. After the service they came over specially to say a shy goodbye.

They remembered the day when I had hovered hesitantly over their prostrate and exhausted bodies and then flown off, only to be prompted to return and rescue them in their extremity.

'We have you to thank for our lives,' commented one, quietly.

Mary and I were unable to reply.

'There was another who also pulled us clear of the mud,' she continued. 'I'm afraid I think he died. I did not know him. He was a Hupla warrior. Even an Elder.'

Two Bible verses from the Gospel of Matthew which had been read out by a Dani tribesman at Gary's funeral came into my mind. They are often read at remembrance day services in November in England.

'Greater love has no man than he lay down his life for his friends.'

Perhaps, I thought, this man was a warrior who understood something of this love. Perhaps. Only the Master himself would know.

Postscript

At the close of 1989, six months after the earthquake, the
Indonesian government announced a transhipment and
re-settlement programme for the inhabitants of the Desa
valley. This meant evacuating the whole Hupla population to Elelim, a centre lower down in the central highlands, about seventy miles (by air) to the north.

Whilst the humanitarian objective of sparing the Hupla
more earthquake disasters was evident, the seismological
risk is considered to be small, compared with the staggering impact that losing 'their' valley was to have on the
displaced Hupla.

No one was forced, but many people were encouraged,
to go to the new location by the entreaties of the Hupla
District Leader (who is *not* called Kwalogo), the 'Kepala
Desa' in Indonesian. A man of uncertain motives, he had
adopted a common 'cargo cult' principle as his rule of life,
and the offer of free, tin-roof accommodation, as much
rice as he could eat, and various other enticements by the
government was enough to swing him behind the move.
Though not loved much by the people, he was able to
persuade some six hundred initially, with the same
inducements (and to be fair, the background of a fatal
disaster), to take up the offer of a free government Puma
helicopter ride to Elelim.

In the event, though, the conditions at Elelim have
proved not only different, but dangerous. Lower down

(365 metres as opposed to 1,700 metres above sea level) the transhipped Hupla began to suffer badly from malaria and dysentery. A recent missionary report notes fifteen people have died and forty-five needed hospitalization after only six months on site. In addition, many of the government offers remain unfulfilled, their intentions often being unmatched by their efficiency.

By 1990 some five hundred of the six hundred transhipped had walked home back to their valley in the mountains. A march of over 150 miles on the trail. Sue Trenier writes from Soba:

'I can only describe the health of those who have returned as pathetic. Many arrived back starved, diseased and exhausted. They now have the difficult problem of settling back in, sick, with little or nothing, and with the uncomfortable memory of parting, often with jibes and harsh words. They are too weak to make gardens so they will share those of the "stayers". The church has much to do to heal these wounds.'

The government had recently announced that not only the Hupla, but some thirty thousand other tribesmen in the same region, including the still battling Husage and Seip, must also be moved.

The missionaries are doing their best to temper these rulings, in so far as they can, with reports to their organizations, and letters to the government offices in Jakarta, Java (two thousand miles away).

In January 1991 Sue wrote on a note of hope:

'The Kepala Desa has been replaced! The government have shown him the door and, in response to the clear leadership that the church elders showed during the emergency, have appointed one of them in his stead. I have great hopes for this man's wisdom and leadership. Also, at last, the restored gardens around Soba are once again beginning to bear fruit, and some sense of the previous economy is returning. Pray for us.'

BARONESS COX
Voice of the Voiceless

Andrew Boyd

Whether in the cellars of Nagorno Karabakh where enemy missiles rain down, the foxholes of Sudan, or the mine-strewn jungles of Burma, Baroness Cox is never far from the frontline.

She is a tireless campaigner for human rights around the world, often risking her life to gather first-hand evidence that will spell-bind and stir the conscience. Hers is one of the great untold adventures of our time.

'As William Wilberforce was a voice for the voiceless and stood against his party and fellow parliamentarians in his campaign to end the slave trade in 18th-century England, so is Baroness Caroline Cox. With true Christian compassion fused with fierce courage, Lady Cox continues to shun mere observation for frontline participation.'

Charles Colson, Wilberforce Award citation,
Washington, USA

ISBN 0 7459 3735 7

KRISS AKABUSI ON TRACK

Ted Harrison

The gripping life story of Olympic hurdler
Kriss Akabusi—a tale of tragedies, temptations and
success.

Ted Harrison traces Kriss's story, from the early
separation from his Nigerian parents and his fostering
in England to the discovery of his royal heritage and
his sporting triumphs. Everything about Kriss
Akabusi is somehow larger than life. This is the
extraordinary story of an extraordinary man.

ISBN 0 7459 2239 2

KING OF THE CON-MEN
The Doug Hartman Story

Doug Hartman with Roger Day

How did a driver in the BBC war correspondent unit
and assistant to Richard Dimbleby end up with a
35-year sentence for a series of over 1,000 frauds?
    The incredible story of the man who triggered
major operational changes in the nation's financial
institutions and how a life of crime brought the
former con-man, dubbed King Con, more than he
bargained for . . .

ISBN 0 7459 3123 5

CLIFF RICHARD: THE BIOGRAPHY

Steve Turner

The revealing new biography of one of the world's top entertainers.

Rock journalist Steve Turner interviewed nearly 200 people closely involved in Cliff's life and career, and also had unparalleled access to Cliff and his management.

'I found Steve's book a really good read.'
Cliff Richard in Hello Magazine

ISBN 0 7459 2789 0

All Lion books are available from your local bookshop, or can be ordered direct from Lion Publishing. For a free catalogue, showing the complete list of titles available, please contact:

Customer Services Department
Lion Publishing plc
Peter's Way
Sandy Lane West
Oxford OX4 6HG
Tel: (01865) 747669
Fax: (01865) 715152

Our website can be found at:
www.lion-publishing.co.uk